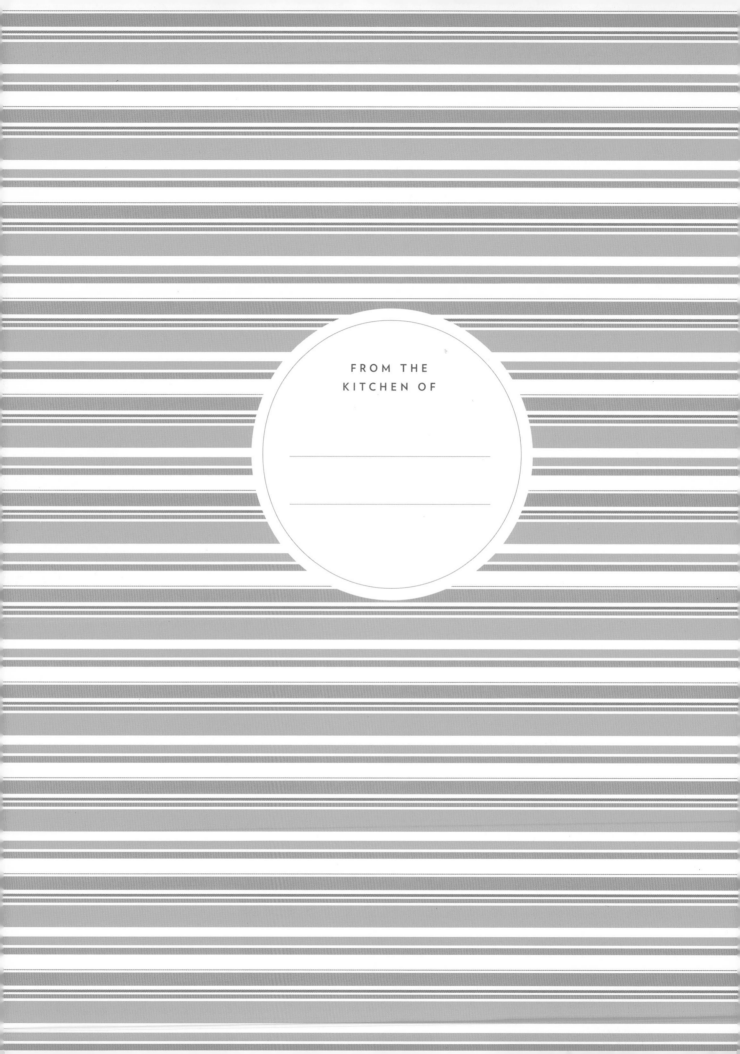

FROM THE
KITCHEN OF

_____

_____

DELICIOUS™
FLAVORS

BY VICTORIA AMORY

PHOTOGRAPHY BY ERIC STRIFFLER

CASA
ROTA

For my boys

LIBRARY OF CONGRESS

PHOTOGRAPHY BY ERIC STRIFFLER

DESIGN BY ANGIE GUBLER AND KRISTIN REES OF BLONDE DESIGNS

COPYRIGHT ©VICTORIA AMORY 2008

ISBN: 1-59975-759-1

PRINTED IN UNITED STATES

DELICIOUS™
FLAVORS

BY VICTORIA AMORY

PHOTOGRAPHY BY ERIC STRIFFLER

CASA
ROTA

CONTENTS

THANK YOU 9

INTRODUCTION 10

ENTERTAINING

① Welcome Weekend Guests **16**

② Easy Everyday Dinner **20**

③ Lunch in the Herb Garden **24**

④ Children's Birthday Party **28**

⑤ Dinner in the Library **32**

⑥ Sunday Lunch by the Fire **36**

MENUS FOR ENTERTAINING 40

RECECIPES

① Drinks 42

② Tapas 56

③ Soups 74

④ Sauces 96

⑤ Salads 118

⑥ Main Courses 138

⑦ Side Dishes 164

⑧ Desserts 186

GUIDE 210

INDEX 212

THANK YOU

Giving thanks is an integral part of entertaining. Thank you notes, after all, are the sign of a great hostess and a superb guest. Here, I wish to thank everyone who helped me create this book.

Eric Striffler and his beautiful photography can turn everyday ingredients into works of art. His artistry, eye and knowledge of all things beautiful are clear in these sophisticated photographs.

Angie Gubler and Kristin Rees from Blonde Designs created the wonderful layouts and made reading recipes over and over again a delight. Style and taste, so essential in cooking and entertaining, have merged here to create these beautiful pages.

Kathleen Hackett helped edit the recipes and asked the right questions to get the right answers. Her input was invaluable.

Leigh Brown Perkins helped organize my ideas into comprehensible paragraphs and turned not so pretty sentences into beautiful prose. Thank you Leigh for all your help. An accomplished freelance writer, Leigh is now working on her own children's book.

Lori Cory helped me every day with a million details and held my hand, the frying pan and the telephone at the same time. Talk about multi-tasking!

We are so proud (and I speak in the royal we) to have printed this book in the USA.

All mistakes are my own.

LIKE MOST PASSIONATE HOME COOKS, I HAVE COME TO THINK OF MY COLLECTION OF RECIPES as a kind of diary, a keepsake bound by shared meals. I can recall details of the faces and places associated with each one, no matter how many years or miles may have passed. The same is probably true of you. And, like you, many of the recipes I adore are influenced by the places I have lived. I was born and raised in Spain, so many of my best food memories mix Andalusian country cooking with elegant Basque cuisine. I have always been inspired by Southern Europe and the Mediterranean diet is my favorite way to eat. I went to school in England, where I spent wonderful weekends at friends' houses drooling over food prepared by their talented mothers. And I now live in America, the source of many of my delicious and practical recipes.

I mix and match dishes, which results in an eclectic rotation of meals. Sometimes they are all American, others Italian, other times pure Spanish or typical French. But more often than not, I take a little of this and a little of that: Spanish tapas, followed by French soup, Italian pasta and then an American dessert. After all, this is why America is so appealing — its blending of many backgrounds and diverse flavors. It makes for memorable meals.

Such cooking connects me with my personal past, vividly remembered, but also with an unknowable past that lingers in the core of my being. When I stir a pot of *potaje*, I think of the millions of other women who have been in my exact position, giving their best to the people they love. The sound of a spoon swirling in a pot belongs to every generation, every home, everywhere. But it is more than a means of providing sustenance. Cooking is my way of calming down, of de-stressing, of grasping reality and of showing love, as much as it is about offering gastronomic pleasure.

This book is my attempt to share my love of home cooking. It is about the passion I have for flavorful, healthy and easy-to-make dishes. Within these pages is my philosophy of cooking, some of my best dishes, plenty of great ideas. I encourage you to follow the recipes, but then make them your own and use them to improve and enhance what you already know. I hope to entice you to transform the daily task of feeding family and friends into a glorious event. Cooking should be magical, exciting and, above all, a pleasure.

I learned to cook by reading books — lots of books — but I wasn't particularly discriminating: One of my earliest solo kitchen adventures was to make, from start to finish, the recipe booklet that came with the food processor. Here is what I learned from that experience: If you can read you can cook.

In my early twenties, when I moved to New York from Madrid and lived in a tiny studio apartment off Beekman Place, cooking became a necessity when I wanted to entertain my friends. I was so proud of living on my own! I remember calling my parents' cook in the country and furiously writing down instructions on how to make my favorite recipes. Any kind of pasta dish was perfect for that tiny kitchen of mine and my two pots. My efforts may not have been as successful as I imagined — I later learned that my friends used to have dinner before coming over!

Practice does make perfect, but perfection has never been my purpose for entertaining or cooking at home. More often than not, I like recipes to take on their own flavors and texture from what is at hand, rather than obsessively following instructions. I learned a few cooking techniques and developed those to fit my taste, budget and availability of ingredients.

Being a self-taught cook and not a professional chef actually allows me the freedom to take chances in the kitchen, to experiment with ingredients today, just as I did with my two little pots near Beekman Place. Home cooking is not about perfection. It is about comforting those I cook for and putting guests at ease. Keeping it stress-free and fun for me makes it a pleasure to have people gathered around my table.

The recipes I always fall back on are the tried-and-true ones. They work because they are simple, full of flavor and elegant. Entertaining for a crowd is not so very different from everyday cooking. Quantities vary and practicality must win out. But having an array of favorite recipes will make your life in the kitchen so much easier and your friends giddy with excitement when they open the mailbox and see an invitation from you.

Starting with good, healthy and fresh ingredients is a must. Ingredients need not be expensive, but they must be of excellent quality to achieve desirable results. The knowledge of transforming humble ingredients into extravagant dishes is one of the, if not the most, important attributes of the home cook.

My schedule allows me to write articles and columns for newspapers and magazines, appear on television, organize charity events, invite friends for dinners and spend time with my family. It does not, however, allow me time to fret over a hot stove, spend endless hours going from one grocery store to another or search the web for rare ingredients. Most of my everyday cooking is done in under an hour, leaving slow-to-cook dishes and roasts for when I entertain larger groups. Those hands-off dishes are the backbone of graceful entertaining. While the oven does the cooking, I have time to set the table and prepare the rest of the meal.

Working at home allows me to plan meals with that in mind. I am able to organize myself by making some things ahead of time and leaving little for the last minute. In the heat of the moment, the phone will ring, the children will demand my attention and there will be a delivery at the door. I have burned bread and overcooked a sauce. And I know that if I leave a lot of finishing touches for last minute, they will just not get done.

I learned how to cook as a young wife because I had to — it was almost like culinary instinct took over me. Cooking meals for my husband was (and is) my way of nurturing and caring for him. When my children were born, another set of skills developed and my food memories became the guiding light. I wanted to duplicate the aromas, feelings and flavors of the food I had growing up in Southern Spain. That is what I want to share with you and my children: respect for good food, memories of extraordinary meals, and the sensibility of eating well.

I cherish recipes that have history; their reason for being is my reason for making them. Within this book there are some stories that, hopefully, will inspire you and explain why I adore making these dishes over and over again. These are my classics. The ones friends and family always ask for, the ones that are memories of wonderful moments and great meals. And if you look carefully at the classics, the ones that are always popular, comforting and safe, it is because they are real and true. Stick to them, enhance them, play with them, tweak them to make them your own and your kitchen will be a source of comfort and inspiration, a refuge and a haven. In other words: home.

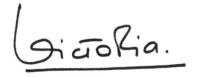

Welcome Weekend Guests

EVERY GOOD HOSTESS knows what to do to make a guest's stay wonderful. I always put myself in my traveling friend's shoes — what would I want upon on arrival? If the trip is short, a chilled beverage is all I need. If the journey involves air travel and accompanying jet lag, I never want to sit through an elaborate meal — I would be exhausted. A warm soup or tasty frittata is an ideal offering. I always have two or three more substantial dishes semi-prepared on hand in the refrigerator in the event a guest is, indeed, eager to sit down to more than one course.

If you think back on your most memorable house visit, chances are the meals are what come to mind first. The room you sleep in is likely the second thing you remember fondly. Even though I have a house full of children, some of my city-dwelling friends prefer a bed in my house to anything else perhaps because there's always the aroma of good food in the air and the pool is just steps away!

A lady of grand consequence once told me that she slept once a year in each of her guest rooms to make sure they were as comfortable as hers. She did have a few houses, actually palaces, and I am sure that each bedroom was as well-appointed as hers.

To make the guest room comfortable and cozy, spend time in the room, carefully look around to insure that everything is as it should be. Turn on all the lamps and lights and replace dead light bulbs. Sit on the bed and in the chair to detect squeaks, lumps or anything that might cause discomfort. Open and close curtains and windows and draw the shades up and down — there's nothing worse than having to fiddle with a stubborn Roman shade. Check to make sure there are enough hangers in the closet and an empty chest of drawers, so that guests can fully unpack rather than live out of their suitcases. Place a scented candle or a bowl with pot-pourri, fresh flowers, a pad of paper and a mint julep cup filled with pencils by the phone, and stock the bathroom with piles of clean towels. When I am a weekend guest, I love to have interesting books and magazines at my fingertips — it's always a welcoming touch. Luxury comes in many guises — my version is not about showy things — I think the details are important. Matching sets of sheets, pillows and bedspreads come to mind. It's not necessary to have gold-plated hardware or windows covered in silk taffeta, but new soap in pretty soap dishes, a hairdryer that works and drawers lined in scented paper are.

No matter the comforting touches, home-cooked meals will always make your guests feel coddled. Keep the menus simple. If you feed them well, they'll always be happy.

Easy Everyday Dinner

EATING TOGETHER, SHARING FOOD and sitting at a table is the best way to create and maintain friendships and togetherness. Rituals, traditions and customs are what unite us as families and clans; it is instinctive and primordial. Elevating everyday dinners to dinner party status is my way of making the job of feeding my family an enjoyable event. So, I say, if dinner parties are such fun to organize, why not plan one every night for your family and close friends? We are all creatures of habit and by making eating together a "habit" it then becomes the norm.

I am not suggesting that you put together a six-course meal on a weeknight, nor do I think that family meals should cause stress for the cook or the commensals. In fact, I strongly suggest that you save making elaborate dishes like a three-layered chocolate soufflé cake when your gourmand friends come to visit. On the other hand, a little effort goes a long way and the more you entertain, the easier it becomes.

For stress-free entertaining, choose menus that don't demand lots of your attention as they cook. Stews, chowders, chili and potages are ideal candidates because they take a few minutes to prepare and a few hours to cook on their own. These dishes call for some chopping and little else. If you cook them for just one hour, they are delicious, but if the phone rings and your attention is diverted for another hour, they will probably taste even better. For side dishes, serve up no-fuss items such as a green salad and sliced tomatoes, a plate of cheeses and warm bread. Dessert can be fruit, minimally prepared.

Have one or two dishes in your repertoire and elaborate on them as you become more comfortable. If you adore making macaroni and cheese, by all means do so! Serve it with a fresh green salad and some store-bought brownies for stress-free entertaining. Your friends are going to be thrilled to be with you in your house and will appreciate any effort you make.

My latest passion for family dinners is Moroccan tagines, which is both the name of the dish as well as the vessel it is made in. A tagine is a conical-shaped earthenware pot that cooks meats, chicken or fish slowly, and I mean slooooowly. It is a snap to use and the outcome is so delicious that tagines have now become a staple in my kitchen. The small amount of meat needed for the tagines, corresponds with my dietetic philosophy of "eat less food." Seasoned and served alongside richly flavored vegetables, spicy, rich tagines make full, satisfying meals.

Lunch in the Herb Garden

ONE OF MY PERSONAL LUXURIES — and one that I urge everyone to try — is to plant a small herb garden. Not much space is needed; a window sill, a few pots in a sunny corner or a small patch just outside the kitchen door is enough to put fresh herbs in your hands whenever you need them. Planting and growing them is very easy to do — and incredibly satisfying.

In Palm Beach, I have planted a small patch on the east side of the house with basil, sage, parsley, chives, oregano, rosemary and mint. Pomegranate, citruses and banana trees shade the herb patch and yield a delicious bounty of fresh fruit. I have planted artichokes, eggplants and Brussels sprouts with little success, but the rosemary bush is thriving, the basil plant has now become a small tree and the lavender is yielding beautiful long stalks.

In Southampton, the herb patch is enhanced with tomatoes, zucchini and string beans. It seems very bucolic and rural, but it is the core of many of my recipes and how I love to cook. On weekends there, I like to scour nurseries for hard-to-find herbs and vegetables like cinnamon-scented basil, lemon verbena and bay leaf. I make these herbs part of our meals and store the overabundance in the freezer to share with my friends when they visit.

Serving lunch in the herb garden is a great way to show off my accomplishments as an amateur gardener! The menu is always based on the profusion of herbs and fruits I've grown myself, but it would be just as delicious if I procured them from the nearest farm stand.

I like to set the table simply when eating outside; it allows the greenery to become the focal point. I need nothing more than a green tablecloth, white plates and simple rattan accessories to set my garden table. My centerpiece is right in front of me — in the herb garden. I cut a generous bunch of mixed herbs and place them in a vase.

I typically invite friends to arrive for lunch at 1 o'clock; we usually don't sit to eat for a good fifteen minutes, though. This allows for a relaxed meal but also shows that you respect guests' busy lives — everyone has appointments and errands to attend to and however much I would like to linger at the table, I believe that lunches should be speedier than dinners. Because the herb garden is in a semi-sunny area, I place sun hats on the backs of chairs for my friends. I don't want to have to get up and move to another spot and spoil the conversation.

Children's Birthday Party

INVITING A GROUP of rambunctious children to an afternoon party at home is actually a pleasure — yes, a pleasure. I survive by keeping the party outside in the garden and by the pool. There is nothing like lots of physical activities to keep everyone exhausted and happy.

Indicate on the invitation that parents are to stay for the duration. Unless you have organized lots of extra help, it is not fair to yourself to have to oversee other people's children, take photos of the blowing of candles and worry about stray chocolate crumbs on the carpet, all at the same time. It's about being a hostess, not a superwoman.

You would be surprised how willing parents are to suffer the chaos of a child's party when they know hors d'oeuvres and a glass of white wine is in the offing (lacing the pink lemonade with a little vodka isn't a bad idea, either!). Plan to offer something a little more sophisticated than peanut butter and jelly sandwiches. In truth, I never serve PB&Js anyway, since nut allergies have become all too common among children. While on the food subject, don't think that children will appreciate a three-layer mille-feuille-double-caramel petit four. Make foods they recognize, just better. In addition to some savory and sweet dishes, offer a fruit platter stocked with grapes, strawberries and melon and incorporate some color by slipping in a few green leaves here and there, especially into sandwiches.

Unless you are the ultimate baker, rely on professionals to make cakes. A triple-chocolate four-tier birthday cake might impress the captive parents, but it will mean nothing to your child that you slaved in the kitchen for days to make it. All they will remember is the figurine that decorates the cake. Trust me. Be inclusive with your guest list and invite if possible your child's whole class to avoid hurt feelings and misunderstandings; siblings should always be welcome. Keep the party short and sweet; two hours of planned activities is perfect. It's fine if your good friends want to linger, but do state on the invitation the beginning and end of the party. Especially the end. Include your children in making, writing and mailing invitations. Ask their input in planning the menu and let them choose their birthday cake. They can also help decorate the garden with balloons and put together a treasure hunt if so inclined. And yes, they should also help with writing thank-you notes. All these events are great teaching tools: with the enticement of the present comes the responsibility of the thank-you note.

Remember that this is supposed to be fun so take lots of photos and keep it short; these are the memories your children will have forever.

ENTERTAINING

Dinner in the Library

SETTING A TABLE for a dinner party should not be exclusive to the dining room, nor should the lack of a dining room stop you from inviting friends for a meal. Many houses today are designed with a multitude of spaces perfectly suited for a sit-down dinner. The table is clearly important, but sharing a meal with family and friends is even more so.

I often set tables in the foyer, particularly when the dining room table becomes a work surface for my sons' art projects, or in the living room when the guest list exceeds the dining room's capacity. And, believe it or not, I've used the driveway when the guest list was really long! If you live in an apartment, where space is at a premium, you really must be clever about how to stage a sit-down meal. Your home office or the playroom are fine places to do this. When I lived in a tiny apartment in New York, we used to sit on banquettes around the bed, and in my first country house, everyone had to bring their own chair to my dinners because my budget at the time only allowed me to purchase a table!

Moving the table around allows me to use all different corners of our house. Sometimes I like to sit by the bay window, at others near the fireplace and still other times it is fun to sit in the garden or in the living room next to the Christmas tree. I am not afraid to invite friends into our bedroom — it brings back fond memories of my early days in New York. For a Sunday night supper, eating in the kitchen is the biggest thrill.

Before we redesigned our current house, I entertained in a dining room that was very small; it barely had enough room for a table of eight. Knowing my entertaining likes and dislikes, we merged three contiguous rooms together, fitted bookcases around the perimeter and placed two round tables in the space to create a dining room/library. Now, we eat surrounded by books in the coziest room in the house.

To set the table for a dinner party, use two main colors. Investing in a white linen tablecloth and napkins will allow you to add color and texture with decorations and accessories. Alternatively, begin your entertaining life with a great set of white plates to mix and match with other colors as you grow your collection. Keep it basic and simple and use the things you have at home in lieu of flowers. It makes for individual and personal decorations and tablesettings.

A simple silver bowl in the center of the table filled with seasonal objects like fruits, pinecones, Christmas balls or even shells is always perfect. Place a group of candlesticks with white or beige tapers in the center of the table for a very elegant look; little else is needed for a clean and classic table.

Sunday Lunch by the Fire

THE COZINESS AND COMFORT of a Sunday at home is the perfect antidote to a stressful week. Being home is great, but sharing a casual lunch there with friends is even better. The key to keeping it relaxed is to choose a low-labor menu. Weekend cooking and entertaining is all about speediness and ease, along with a huge dose of practicality.

I don't mind spending precious weekend time over the stove, but only if it will make my life easier later in the week, meaning I can enjoy two meals from one cooking session. I often use leftovers of those grand Sunday lunches to last me a few days during the week. If I am cooking, I might as well make the best of it and double recipes that freeze well or last for a few days in the refrigerator.

Inviting friends for Sunday lunch forces me to cook (something I adore to do in any case) and have a few ideas for meals and recipes for the following days.

Setting the table in the kitchen can be as sophisticated and elegant as you like, or as casual as you want to be. I like to incorporate a bit of both: the buffet is arrayed on the kitchen table and guests sit in the living room by the fire with plates on their laps. The entertainment is the mesmerizing fire.

I adore winter lunches that can feed ten or twenty people. Especially on days like New Year's, the day after Thanksgiving or Boxing Day when I never know how many people will trickle in for a warm meal. The comfort of sitting by the fire with a plate of delicious food on my lap, surrounded by family and friends, is to me what the art of entertaining is meant to be.

Use large plates and large napkins when serving food buffet-style. This is not because you want to encourage piling on the food but to avoid spillage; the larger the plate the less chance of a ruined rug. Large napkins cover your lap and part of your knees — always a good idea when sitting on a low chair or the floor. At home I do serve red wine though I know that most people don't. My philosophy: It's Sunday, a day to relax and indulge. Place decanters filled with white and red wine and pitchers with Bullshots or Bloody Marys on the buffet table or sideboard to make self-service easy on you and comfortable for your guests.

Make it simple, especially on those spur-of-the-moment weekend extravaganzas, by enlisting the help of a single male friend. I know they are hard to come by but they are eternally grateful for a home-cooked meal and will do almost anything to get invited back. Asking for their help in setting up the bar, lighting the fire and mixing drinks is a brilliant way to get it all done.

MENUS FOR ENTERTAINING

(1) **WELCOME WEEKEND GUESTS**
Make-Ahead Menu for a Relaxed Dinner with Friends

Champagne & Pomegranate PAGE 52

Huevos al Plato PAGE 144

Boneless Leg of Lamb a la Moruna PAGE 162

Baby Bok Choy with Roasted Garlic PAGE 177

Bread & Butter Pudding with Pedro Ximénez PAGE 197

(2) **EASY EVERYDAY DINNER**
A Touch of the Exotic to Cheer up the Middle of the Week

Caipirinha PAGE 49

Tomato Salad PAGE 132

Tagine of Chicken, Olives & Lemon PAGE 155

Smashed Potatoes with Rosemary PAGE 173

Banana Ice Cream PAGE 209

(3) **LUNCH IN THE GARDEN**
Fresh Green Herbs for a Ladylike Lunch

Southampton Iced Tea PAGE 51

Patatas Bravas PAGE 72

Prawns en Papillote PAGE 148

Basil Ice Cream PAGE 208

Strawberry & Cointreau Sauce PAGE 193

MENUS FOR ENTERTAINING

(4) CHILDREN'S BIRTHDAY PARTY
A Blissful Afternoon in the Garden for All

Vodka & Watermelon *(Vodka-less for the Children)* PAGE 52

Meatballs with Mint PAGE 70

Potato Tortilla with Onions & Chorizo PAGE 66

Orange Pound Cake with Lemon Curd PAGE 199

Fried Cookies PAGE 201

(5) DINNER IN THE LIBRARY
An Elegant Dinner to Impress Your Nearest and Dearest

Potato Crisps PAGE 71

Smoked Salmon Soup PAGE 87

Chicken in Champagne Sauce PAGE 156

Garden Vegetables with Tarragon Butter PAGE 183

Chocolate Crêpe Cake PAGE 202

(6) SUNDAY LUNCH BY THE FIRE
Comfort and Coziness for the Best Day of the Week

Eggplant Bundles with Goat Cheese PAGE 181

Good Old-Fashioned Meat Loaf PAGE 160

Smashed Peas with Mint PAGE 184

Mashed Potatoes en Croûte PAGE 174

Orange Bread & Butter Pudding PAGE 198

Drinks

Carajillo, PAGE 46

Bullshot, PAGE 47

Caipirinha & Caipiroska, PAGE 49

Southside, **PAGE 50**

Southampton Iced Tea, PAGE 51

Vodka & Watermelon, PAGE 52

Champagne & Pomegranate, PAGE 52

Sangría de Verdad, PAGE 54

The Wake-Up-Call, PAGE 55

Tinto de Verano, PAGE 55

ANDALUCIA, WITH ITS DEEP ROMAN ROOTS AND MOORISH INFLUENCES, IS THE LAND OF FLAMENCO MUSIC, BULLFIGHTING AND DARK-EYED

ladies with carnations tucked in their hair. But it is also touched by a heavy dose of Anglomania. Many old-fashioned British traditions exist there to this day. Perhaps we have sherry to thank for that. The sherry industry, centered in Jerez de la Frontera, Sanlúcar de Barrameda and El Puerto de Santa Maria, is as booming today as it was in the 17th century, when the export of sherry wines and brandy established an enduring connection with England.

British savoir-faire may be considered the ultimate in elegance, but transported to southern Spain that elegance receives a strong dose of Spanish fun. What results is an explosive concoction of propriety and hilarity — the British stiff upper lip meets the nonchalant *mañana* culture. This oddly charming mixture is most apparent in this chapter, where classic British cocktails are given a touch of Spanish *alegría*.

My own education in libations was nearly a birthright. My godfather, Alfonso Domecq, of the notable sherry family, was married to my father's sister Silvia. They were my favorite aunt and uncle, she incredibly charming and beautiful, he so attractive and debonair. Every year I would spend a few days with them in Jerez, where I visited bodegas, sipped extraordinary wines and brandies and walked among chalk-marked barrels dating from the 1700s. I saw Napoleon's signature, Empress Eugenia's personal barrel of wine and watched in awe as the catador dispensed a perfect serving of sherry from a barrel with a mere flip of his wrist.

Many classic drinks and certain foods of Andalucia were inherited from the British, then changed to suit the tastes of the Andalucian people. They remain, however, in essence, totally British. We sipped minted iced tea on warm summer afternoons, had Bullshots on chilly winter mornings before partridge shoots and made Bloody Marys before grand Sunday lunches. We didn't really need an occasion for raising a glass, though. Growing up, a visit from the Domecq cousins always meant a heavy round of drinks and loads of fun.

The other drinks in this chapter are the ones I serve at home. Some are based on classic combinations like Carajillo, a delicious coffee and brandy mixture, and others are perfect entertaining drinks that can be made in larger quantities. Please be careful when drinking alcohol and plan for a designated driver.

The most successful parties are those in which a special drink, a "house drink," is served. It instantly sets the mood and makes guests immediately feel welcome. I am a big fan of serving cocktails mixed in large glass pitchers rather than stirring up individual drinks. I toss pitchers together just before the party is to begin, chill them in the refrigerator and set them out on the bar on a gleaming silver or lacquered tray when the doorbell rings. This way, I can simply pour a drink without much fanfare. Your "house special" doesn't have to be anything complicated — though it can be. Some of my favorites are in this chapter, but other simple concoctions like pineapple and rum or freshly squeezed orange juice and vodka are also delicious. Serve them with easy-to-make tapas or just salted nuts, olives and cubes of manchego cheese.

Carajillo

Carajillo, literally translated, means little courage. It is said this cocktail originated during the Spanish-Cuban War, when soldiers would drink it to gain a little courage before battle. In Spain, this brandy and coffee combination is a popular indulgence on both chilly winter and cool summer mornings. It is the drink of choice before setting out on a hunt or before any other rural pursuit— a Carajillo is what gives you that oomph to be brave and face the day. For winter lunches in Southampton, I move the cocktail hour to dessert by pouring the mixture over vanilla ice cream. There is simply no easier-to-make—or better loved—ending to a meal.

2 cups espresso coffee, freshly made and very hot

½ cup brandy

2 tablespoons sugar

In a pitcher, combine the coffee, brandy and sugar. Stir gently to dissolve the sugar. Pour into demitasse or hot toddy cups or mugs and serve.

MAKES 6 DRINKS

Bullshot

This close relative of the Bloody Mary was my father's favorite drink. He always ordered one at the legendary King Cole Bar in the St. Regis Hotel during his visits to New York. It is there that the Bloody Mary as we know it today was born. This concoction is an especially sensational prelude to a long, leisurely lunch on a cold day. Make it with good quality organic beef broth, and season it to taste with freshly ground black pepper. Add a splash of tomato juice to the glass to create another Bloody Mary relation, the "Bloody Bull."

4 cups Beef Stock, page 101

1 tablespoon Worcestershire sauce

1 teaspoon fresh ground pepper

Juice of 1 lemon

2 cups vodka

In a 2-quart pitcher, combine the broth, Worcestershire sauce, pepper and lemon juice. Stir until incorporated. Add the vodka and stir again. Fill 6 double old-fashioned glasses with ice and pour the Bullshot mixture into each one.

MAKES 6 DRINKS

Caipirinha & Caipiroska

I first had this drink on a trip to Rio de Janeiro where we traveled for my older brother's wedding. Here is the authentic recipe made with Cachaça, Brazil's local spirit. It is said that Cachaça was once strictly used for medicinal purposes; that may well be, as it is very strong and goes straight to your head! Dilute it with equal parts water if you like. Another less-potent version of this refreshing Brazilian drink, the Caipiroska, is made with vodka rather than Cachaça.

Traditionalists may scoff at my making either one by the pitcherful as they are always made individually, but who has time for that? These are always popular, so make several batches, and stir in the alcohol just before serving.

6 limes, each cut into 8 wedges

1 cup sugar

12 ounces Cachaça or vodka

Ice cubes

In a large pitcher, combine the limes and the sugar and muddle with a wooden spoon or muddler until the sugar dissolves. Add the Cachaça or vodka and stir to combine. Fill a cocktail shaker with ice and pour in the liquid. Shake. To serve, pour into ice-filled glasses.

MAKES 6 DRINKS

Southside

This classic Long Island drink always takes me to Southampton, no matter where I serve it. Its mix of rum, mint, sugar and lemon juice is summer in a glass. I personally prefer this drink made with vodka rather than rum; you be the judge. Better yet, make a pitcher of each and let your friends decide!

½ cup rum or vodka

Juice of 1 lime

1 cup simple syrup

1 sprig fresh mint, stems removed

Crushed ice

Lime wedges for garnish

In a 2-quart blender filled halfway with ice, combine the rum, gin or vodka, lime juice, simple syrup and mint leaves. Blend until smooth. Pour into highball glasses and garnish with a lime.

MAKES 2 DRINKS

HOW TO MAKE SIMPLE SYRUP

In a large heat-proof pitcher or glass, mix equal parts of sugar and boiling water until sugar dissolves. Chill before using.

Southampton Iced Tea

My husband Minot introduced me to this classic Long Island drink, a refreshing mix of tea, orange juice and mint. It is the drink at golf courses in Southampton. I make it at home and leave it in pitchers in the refrigerator, so that it is always on hand. For elegant ladies' lunches, I serve it in large crystal pitchers; it is the color of a beautiful summer sunset and it goes with almost any lunch menu. Spiked with rum or alcohol-free, it is refreshing and deliciously sweet. Use fresh, good ingredients and make the tea from scratch.

4 Earl Grey or British Breakfast tea bags or 4 tablespoons loose tea

½ cup fresh orange juice

½ cup fresh mint leaves (plus extra sprigs for garnish)

Water

Place the tea bags in a mug. Pour one cup of boiling water over it and steep for at least 10 minutes or until the tea is very strong. Place the mint leaves in a second mug. Pour another cup of boiling water into the mug and steep for about 10 minutes. In a 2-quart pitcher, combine the steeped tea and mint. Add the orange juice and fill with cold water. To serve, pour the tea into tall glasses filled with ice cubes and garnish with fresh mint sprigs.

MAKES 6 TO 8 DRINKS

Vodka & Watermelon

Every kid loves watermelon in the summer, but add a splash of vodka and you have a decidedly grown-up cocktail. Watermelon pairs with any liquor beautifully and here, mixed with vodka and a squeeze of lime, it is as delicious a warm-weather drink as you can find.

1 ripe watermelon, seeded and puréed, about 4 to 5 cups

1 cup vodka

Juice of 2 limes

Strain the watermelon pulp through a fine-mesh strainer to get rid of as much pulp as possible. Combine the watermelon juice, vodka and lime juice in a glass 2-quart pitcher. Fill 6 iced-tea glasses with ice and pour some of the drink into each.

MAKES 6 DRINKS

Champagne & Pomegranate

Who can argue with a drink that combines the health benefits of pomegranates with the effervescence of a little bubbly? The jewel-tone color makes it an ideal holiday offering. What's more, it is easily put together in large pitchers to serve a crowd.

1 cup organic pomegranate juice

Juice of 2 limes, plus more for garnish

1 750-ml bottle of Champagne or sparkling wine such as cava or Prosecco

In a 2-quart glass pitcher, combine the pomegranate juice and lime juice. Slice the limes into thin rounds and float in the juice. Just before serving, add the Champagne. Pour into tall glasses filled with ice. Add a lime slice to each glass for garnish.

MAKES 8 DRINKS

Sangría de Verdad

Among the millions of versions of sangría, this one is the simplest, best and, in my opinion, truest (thus the name "verdad"). To make it authentic, use a red Rioja, the traditional Spanish wine. It is possible to make this drink a day in advance, but I prefer to have all of the ingredients ready and assemble just before serving.

1 orange, seeded and sliced into ¼-inch rounds

1 lemon, seeded and sliced into ¼-inch rounds

1 apple, seeded and sliced into 8 wedges

1 peach, pitted and sliced into 8 wedges

1 750-ml bottle of Rioja or other Spanish red wine

1 cup Cointreau (orange liqueur)

1 16-ounce can lemon-lime soda

In a 2-quart glass pitcher, combine all of the ingredients. Fill 6 to 8 glasses with ice and pour sangría into each. Spoon some of the fruit into each glass for a garnish.

MAKES 6 TO 8 DRINKS

The Wake-Up-Call

When my husband's friends stop by for brunch before a golf game, I often make them this eye-opening drink, which gets its kick from brandy and anise. I like to think I am helping them improve their game, but I am also improving my own prospects because when they tee off after a Wake-Up-Call, I know I'll have at least five solid hours to myself.

2 cups fresh orange juice

½ cup lemon juice

½ cup brandy

1 teaspoon Pernod (anise-flavored liqueur)

In a pitcher, combine all the ingredients. Fill 4 juice glasses with ice and pour the drink into each.

MAKES 4 DRINKS

Tinto de Verano

This "summer wine" is the drink in Andalucia during the summer months. I've long sipped it mixed with Casera, a regional brand of lemon-lime soda that gives this cooling libation a particularly bright flavor. Unfortunately, this soda is becoming increasingly difficult to come by. I have found the closest substitutes are 7UP and Sprite. A generous squeeze of lemon or lime juice makes the difference between a good drink and a superb one.

2 cups red or white wine

2 cups lemon-lime soda

Juice of 2 limes

Combine all the ingredients in a 2-quart pitcher. Fill 6 highball glasses with ice and pour the Tinto de Verano into each.

MAKES 6 DRINKS

Tapas

Garlic Shrimp, PAGE 60

Clams with Chorizo, PAGE 61

Shrimp & Eggplant Bundles, PAGE 62

Fried Eggplantt with Honey, PAGE 63

Chorizo Empanadas, PAGE 64

Pork Tenderloin with Pedro Ximénez & Cabrales Cheese, PAGE 65

Potato Tortilla with Onion & Chorizo, PAGE 66

Serrano-Wrapped Figs with Blue Cheese, PAGE 68

Tomato & Jamón Serrano Toasts with Truffle Oil, PAGE 69

Meatballs with Mint, PAGE 70

Potato Crisps, PAGE 71

Patatas Bravas (Fiery Potatoes), PAGE 72

Spiced Walnuts, PAGE 73

GOING DE TAPEO, OR OUT FOR TAPAS, IS A NATIONAL PASTIME IN SPAIN. IT IS THE WAY TO SOCIALIZE, TASTE

local specialties and whet the appetite for those long, languid Spanish lunches!

In Spain, tapas are never eaten at home but rather in tabernas or bars, and always eaten while standing up. Traditionally, Spaniards eat tapas before lunch, but nowadays also before dinner and always accompanied by local wines or beer. In Andalucia, almost everyone drinks dry sherry or a local white wine such as Barbadillo. At tapas bars, patrons can choose from a long list of specialties written on a blackboard or an array of dishes already cooked in *cazuelas* (earthenware platters) displayed on top of the bar. During the week, Spaniards may stop at one taberna before lunch to sample tiny tastes of something fabulous — and then head off to eat a full lunch. But on Saturday (most places are closed on Sunday), one might go to three or four tapas bars. When I visit, I often go to several tapas bars and skip lunch altogether so I can sample as many dishes as possible!

At home, I like preparing classic tapas recipes and serving them as accompaniments to grilled meats or fish. It is a great way to add flavor and color to menus and introduce new and exotic ingredients in small portions. I like to show off new tapas recipes at a cocktail party or buffet. Almost any dish can be turned into a tapa; the point of it is the size of the portion and the variety of the dishes. Romaine Hearts with Crispy Garlic, page 129, Mussels with Curry Sauce, page 150, and Ensaladilla

Rusa page 137, can be served as tapas if you portion them just so. I've even put little pieces of Chicken Milanese on top of a tiny slice of bread and called it a tapa.

The word tapa means cover and they were traditionally small plates placed on top of a glass of wine so that flies could not get in the wine. It is attributed to King Alfonso X "The Wise" (1211-1284) who, due to a stomach ailment, had to eat small portions of food accompanied by sips of wine. After he recuperated from his illness, he made a decree that all bars had to serve wine with something small to eat. A slice of bread served on top of the wine glass became what bartenders offered. Soon, that piece of bread was enhanced with other tidbits: cured cheese, marinated anchovies, seasoned olives or chorizo and jamón Serrano.

In the Basque country, bites served with a skewer or toothpick are called *pinchos* (from the verb *pinchar:* to prick). In Andalucia, some are called *montaditos,* which are served on top of a piece of bread; but if they have a toothpick they are called *banderillas,* because they resemble the spears at bullfights. *Raciónes* are individual portions and *cazuelitas* are a larger version. Most are finger foods and are served with lots of bread to mop up juices, but sometimes — for the juicier ones — a fork is used.

To serve tapas, you can bring out all the dishes at once or serve them in succession. Offer soup in small cordial glasses, followed by fish dishes, meats, vegetarian plates and cheese. I often prepare an entire meal made up of tapas — 8 to 10 different dishes. However you choose to serve the recipes in this chapter, you will not be disappointed. Some of these recipes are ancient and others represent new trends in Spanish cooking, but all are delicious, easy to make and full of flavor.

Garlic Shrimp

This is one of the best-known tapas and one that appears on every menu in every Spanish restaurant. I often make this at home and serve it as an hors d'oeuvres for a cocktail party. I like these shrimp very garlicky and spicy and use red pepper flakes to duplicate the heat of guindillas, the smoked red chiles from Spain. When I make Garlic Shrimp for a large group, I present them on round earthenware cazuelas along with a basket of warm baguettes to mop up the very spicy juices.

½ cup extra-virgin olive oil

1 head garlic, peeled and sliced

2 tablespoons crushed red pepper flakes

2 pounds jumbo shrimp, deveined and peeled

Sea salt

In a large sauté pan, heat the olive oil over high heat until smoking. Add the garlic and red pepper flakes and sauté until the garlic turns golden, about 2 minutes. Add the shrimp and stir well to coat with the olive oil. Cook until the shrimp are opaque, 2 to 3 minutes. Season with salt and serve very hot.

SERVES 4 AS A MAIN COURSE, 6 TO 8 AS A TAPA

Clams with Chorizo

Chorizo is a divine pork sausage made spicy and hot with pimentón, or paprika. In this dish, the spices from the chorizo impart a wonderfully smoky flavor to the clams and turn the sauce a dazzling red. Add red pepper flakes if the chorizo is not spicy enough or use Cajun sausage if your supermarket doesn't carry the Spanish kind.

2 tablespoons olive oil

1 pound chorizo sausage, sliced into thin rounds

4 cloves of garlic, peeled and chopped

1 cup white wine

3 pounds small Manila, littleneck or cherrystone clams

½ cup finely chopped parsley

Sea salt

Place the clams in a large bowl filled with salted water. Let sit for about 30 minutes, or until it is evident they have released their sand. Repeat a couple of times until there is no sand in the bowl.

In a large sauté pan with a tight-fitting lid, heat the olive oil over medium heat. Add the chorizo and cook until softened and the sides begin to turn crispy. Add the garlic and cook until fragrant, about 1 minute. Add the white wine and deglaze the pan by scraping the bottom to release all the bits. Raise the heat to medium-high, add the clams (do not overcrowd) cover and cook, shaking the pan once in a while until the clams open, 5 to 8 minutes. Transfer the clams and broth to a large, shallow serving dish. Just before serving toss the clams with the parsley.

SERVES 6

Shrimp & Eggplant Bundles

This recipe from Sevilla combines the best of two distinct local ingredients: eggplant from the land and shrimp from the Marismas, the coastal marshland and nature preserve along the Guadalquivir River, which is known for its shellfish.

2 pounds eggplant (about 4 medium)

1 pound jumbo shrimp, peeled and deveined, tails removed

½ cup all-purpose flour

1 large egg, beaten

½ cup plain bread crumbs

Olive oil for frying

Sea salt

Mayonnaise with Mint, page 108

Cut the eggplants in ¼-inch strips lengthwise and place in a shallow, ovenproof dish. Sprinkle with sea salt and set aside for 30 minutes.

Place the eggplant in a colander to rinse. Pat dry with paper towels. Lay a strip of eggplant on a work surface. Center a shrimp at one end and wrap the eggplant around it. Secure with a toothpick. Place the flour on a dinner plate. Next to it, place the beaten egg in a bowl. On another dinner plate, place the bread crumbs. Dredge the rolls first in flour, followed by the egg and the breadcrumbs. Heat the olive oil in a sauté pan over high heat. Working in batches, add the shrimp bundles and sauté until golden on all sides, 3 to 4 minutes. Transfer the shrimp bundles to a paper towel-lined plate to drain. Keep in a warm oven until ready to serve. Place the shrimp bundles on a round platter with the mayonnaise in a small bowl in the center.

MAKES 20

Fried Eggplant with Honey

A classic Andalucian tapa from Cádiz, these thinly sliced and fried eggplants are a staple in most Andalucian kitchens. Compose a lunch of them with two other tapas dishes such as Gambas al Ajillo (Garlic Shrimp, page 60) and Tortilla de Patatas (Potato Tortilla, page 66). I place them all in the middle of the table, family style, for everyone to dig in. Warm crispy baguettes and cold beer are the ideal accompaniments.

4 medium eggplants

Sea salt

½ cup all-purpose flour

½ cup blond or other light-flavored beer

6 tablespoons orange blossom or wildflower honey

Olive oil for frying

Cut the eggplants into thin rounds and place in a shallow pan. Sprinkle with sea salt and set aside for 30 minutes. Rinse in a colander, then pat dry with paper towels.

In a small bowl, combine the flour and beer and mix until smooth. Working in batches, dip the eggplant slices into the batter and coat on both sides. In a medium sauté pan, heat the olive oil over high heat until smoking. Working in batches, fry the eggplants until golden, about 2 minutes per side. Once the first batch is made, reduce the temperature to medium and continue frying the rest of the eggplant slices. Using a slotted spoon, transfer the eggplant to a paper towel-lined plate. Place in a warm oven until ready to serve. Just before serving drizzle with honey.

SERVES 6

Chorizo Empanadas

This version of Mallorcan pastries is made with store-bought frozen puff pastry, making them easy for the home cook. The filling for these particular empanadas happens to be chorizo, hard-boiled eggs and sautéed onions. Some are made with flaky tuna fish and hard-boiled eggs, others with spring vegetables or ground meat and spices.

2 tablespoons olive oil

1 large onion, finely diced

2 cloves of garlic, diced

1 pound chorizo, diced

1 8-ounce can diced tomatoes

½ cup white wine

2 tablespoons fresh oregano, chopped

4 hard-boiled eggs, thinly sliced

Sea salt and fresh ground pepper

2 sheets store-bought frozen puff pastry, thawed

1 egg, beaten

In a sauté pan, heat the olive oil over medium-high heat. Add onions and garlic and sauté until translucent, about 5 minutes. Add the chorizo and cook until it begins to release its juices and becomes slightly golden. Add the tomatoes and wine, bring to a boil, then reduce the heat and simmer until the liquid is evaporated. Add the oregano and season with salt and pepper.

Preheat the oven to 350°F. Line an ovenproof dish with one sheet of puff pastry so that there is about one inch of pastry hanging all around. Pour in the cooked chorizo mixture. Scatter the eggs on top. Top with the second sheet of puff pastry and seal the edges by rolling them with your fingers to create a ridge. Using a fork, make a decorative edge. Brush the top with the beaten egg and, using a sharp knife, make a few decorative slashes on top.

Bake until the pastry turns golden brown, about 30 minutes. Cut into 2-inch squares and serve with Aïoli, page 107, on the side.

SERVES 6 TO 8

Pork Tenderloin with Pedro Ximénez & Cabrales Cheese

I adore the complex flavor of Pedro Ximénez, a sweet dessert sherry, mixed with Cabrales cheese, Spain's blue cheese from the mountains of the Basque country. Slices of pork tenderloin fit perfectly on a slice of baguette so you can make tons of this tapa easily. It is extremely easy to assemble.

4 tablespoons olive oil

Sea salt and fesh ground pepper

2 pork tenderloins

½ cup Pedro Ximénez

1 baguette, thinly sliced

½ pound Cabrales, sliced to fit on top of the tenderloin

Heat the oven to 350°F. Season the tenderloins with salt and pepper. In a large sauté pan, heat the olive oil over high heat until smoking. Add the tenderloins and cook until browned, about 10 minutes per side (30 minutes total). Add the Pedro Ximénez, reduce the heat, and simmer until the sauce thickens and the tenderloins are cooked through, about 10 minutes. Remove from the heat and let the tenderloins rest to allow the juices to reabsorb.

On a cutting board, slice the tenderloins into ¼-inch thick slices. Arrange the baguette slices on a baking sheet and toast until golden, 5 to 6 minutes. Drizzle the tenderloin pan juices over each toast. Place a piece of tenderloin on top of a toasted baguette slice, top with a teaspoon of Cabrales cheese and bake just until the cheese melts, about 3 minutes.

MAKES 15 TO 20

Potato Tortilla with Onion & Chorizo

These potato tortillas are an everyday dish in Spanish households. I make them for the children with only potatoes, but grownups adore this heartier version. In the summer, I serve tortillas with a dollop of creamy Homemade Mayonnaise, page 106, and in the winter with hot Tomato Sauce, page 116. Either way, they are versatile, delicious and economical — the ideal supper dish.

The proportion of eggs to potatoes sparks endless controversy. Some people like it runny (I don't) and some like it totally dry (again, I don't) and it depends on which pan you use, the texture and age of the potatoes and the freshness of the eggs. A friend suggests adding a little milk when scrambling the eggs and another cooks the potatoes to almost-mashed status. This recipe is the most basic and the best, the one with which I have had the most success.

6 medium Idaho potatoes

½ cup olive oil

1 small white onion, diced

2 cups chorizo, diced

6 large eggs

Sea salt

Peel the potatoes and dice them into ½-inch cubes, placing them in a bowl of water with a large pinch of salt while dicing the rest. Using a kitchen towel, pat the potatoes dry. In a large, non-stick frying pan, heat 8 tablespoons of the olive oil over medium-low heat. Add the potatoes and cook until soft but not golden, 15 to 20 minutes. Stir once in a while so they don't stick to the bottom of the pan but be careful not to break them too much.

In a small frying pan, heat 3 tablespoons of olive oil until smoking, lower the heat and add the onions and chorizo. Cook until the chorizo releases its juices and the onions caramelize, about 10 minutes.

Whisk the eggs in a large bowl and add the onion-chorizo mixture and cooked potatoes. Mix well. Return the potato-egg mixture to a well-oiled pan and cook 8 to 10 minutes or until the sides turn golden and you can shake the tortilla. Using a lid or a plate, slide the tortilla onto a plate and flip it back into the pan. Cook 4 to 5 minutes more. Cut into wedges or squares and pass with toothpicks.

SERVES 6

Serrano-Wrapped Figs with Blue Cheese

Some combinations work just as well as a tapa, first course or a dessert. This is one of them. To serve as a tapa, I throw the prepared figs under the broiler for a few seconds just to allow everything to melt slightly. As a first course, I serve the trio over a bed of lettuce drizzled with aged balsamic vinegar and olive oil. As a dessert, I top it with a warm honey and butter sauce. In any case, this combination is sweet, tart and hearty, a great ending or beginning to any meal. *To make it for dessert, melt 1 cup of honey with 2 tablespoons melted butter and drizzle over the figs.

12 fresh figs, halved

6 slices Serrano ham, halved

8 ounces creamy blue cheese like Cambozola or Cabrales

Preheat the oven to 350°F. Place a teaspoon of cheese on top of each fig half. Wrap a piece of ham around the fig and secure with a toothpick.

Arrange the wraps on a cookie sheet lined with parchment paper and bake until cheese melts slightly, about 10 minutes. Serve warm.

MAKES 24

Tomato & Jamón Serrano Toasts with Truffle Oil

Toasted baguette slices or white country bread, rubbed with garlic, topped with fresh slices of tomato and dressed up with jamón Serrano is, in my opinion, the quintessential example of Spanish flavors. Some versions call for infusing the olive oil with garlic and herbs, while others call for slow-roasting the tomatoes to underscore their flavors. Still others call for the tomato to be rubbed onto the bread, which soaks it in yet allows the bread to remain crisp. I adore all versions of this and often serve "pan con tomaca" as a simple tapa at home. For a twist, sprinkle the bread with truffle oil and top it with the classic ingredients. When I serve this, there is never a single piece left on the platter.

2 thin baguettes, sliced into ½-inch thick slices

20 thin slices of jamón Serrano, cut to fit the bread

7 or 8 Roma tomatoes, sliced very thin

4 cloves of garlic, peeled

¼ cup truffle oil

Preheat the oven to 350°F. Rub the baguette slices on one side with garlic and sprinkle with a little truffle olive oil. Place on cookie sheets in a single layer and bake for about 15 minutes, until toasted and golden. Let cool. Top each with one slice of tomato, then drape the Serrano ham over it. Arrange on a shallow platter and serve at room temperature.

MAKES ABOUT 40

Meatballs with Mint

I remember eating these meatballs as a child and, much to my pleasure, they are now a favorite of my children. In my parents' house, they were served with mountains of diced fried potatoes and bowls of buttery peas. I adore these meatballs served with white rice; it absorbs all the delicious sauce. I make them with a combination of ground veal, beef or turkey. But I have also made them with ground lamb when available. The mint gives these meatballs a unique flavor.

2 pounds ground beef, veal or turkey or a combination of all three

½ cup mint, finely chopped

2 tablespoons bread crumbs

1 whole egg

Sea salt and fresh ground pepper

4 tablespoons olive oil

2 cups Salsa Española, page 111

In a large bowl, mix together the ground meats, mint, bread crumbs, egg and salt and pepper. Form into one-inch balls. In a large sauté pan, heat the olive oil until smoking. Cook the meatballs until golden on all sides. Using a slotted spoon, transfer the meatballs to a paper towel-lined plate. Discard all but 1 tablespoon of the oil left in the pan and return the meatballs to the heat. Add the Salsa Española, reduce the heat and simmer until the meatballs are cooked through and the sauce is bubbly, about 10 minutes. Garnish with additional fresh mint.

SERVES 6

Potato Crisps

When I give dinner parties, I often get requests from friends for favorite dishes. My friend Pamela always asks for these oven-fried potatoes and I am happy to oblige by making a huge batch. They don't keep overnight, and some of them do come out a little soggy but I love them nonetheless; you can really tell they are homemade. Serve them with Mayonnaise with Truffle Oil, page 107, or all on their own on a silver plate lined with a linen napkin to elevate lowly potatoes into an extravagant treat.

4 large Idaho potatoes

Sea salt and fresh ground pepper

Olive oil

Preheat the oven to 400°F. Using a mandolin, slice the potatoes widthwise very thinly. Place them in a bowl of cold salted water as you work. Using a kitchen towel, dry the potato slices and arrange them in one layer on cookie sheets lined with parchment paper. Sprinkle olive oil all over the potatoes. Season with sea salt and pepper.

Bake until crisp and golden, about 15 minutes. Serve warm.

SERVES 6 TO 8

Patatas Bravas (Fiery Potatoes)

Every tapas bar serves a version of this dish. This one is my favorite. Roughly cut into rounds and fried, the potatoes are the perfect vehicle for the two spicy sauces. Sometimes the potatoes are cubed and eaten with a toothpick, other times they are cut in wedges. These potatoes must be made just before serving – plan a cold menu of dishes that can be made ahead and add just this one for a hot tapa. Dip the potato in the tomato sauce and then in the mayonnaise for the two sauces to mix in one bite.

4 large potatoes, peeled and sliced into ¼-inch rounds

1 bay leaf

Salt and fresh ground pepper

4 tablespoons olive oil

1 cup Tomato Sauce, page 116

2 tablespoons Dijon mustard

1 cup Homemade Mayonnaise, page 106

1 teaspoon Tabasco sauce or more to taste

Preheat the oven to 400°F. Bring a large pot of salted water to a boil. Add the potato rounds and the bay leaf, and cook until just soft, about 10 minutes. Using a slotted spoon, remove the potatoes from the water and place them in one layer on a cookie sheet lined with parchment paper. Drizzle with olive oil and season with salt and pepper. Bake until golden, 15 to 20 minutes.

In a saucepan, combine the tomato sauce and Dijon mustard; heat through and keep warm until ready to serve. In a small bowl combine the mayonnaise with Tabasco sauce and taste to adjust seasoning.

To serve, arrange the potatoes in the center of a shallow platter. Place the warm tomato sauce on one side and the mayonnaise on the other.

SERVES 6 TO 8

Spiced Walnuts

This is a quick, easy way to dress up walnuts for the cocktail hour. I also use these walnuts as a garnish for soups and sprinkle them on green salads for extra crunch. Pecans and almonds, or a combination of all, are also delicious seasoned this way.

1 tablespoon cayenne pepper

1 tablespoon chopped rosemary

1 tablespoon ground ginger

1 tablespoon sea salt

1 tablespoon paprika

1 cup walnuts

2 tablespoons olive oil

Preheat the oven to 350°F. Combine the cayenne, rosemary, ginger, sea salt and paprika in a medium bowl. Add the walnuts and toss to coat. Add the olive oil and toss to coat well.

Place the nuts on a cookie sheet lined with parchment paper and bake for about 10 minutes until the walnuts become fragrant. Let cool before serving. The nuts will keep for 1 week in an airtight container.

MAKES 1 CUP

Soups

COLD SOUPS

Yellow Gazpacho, PAGE 78

Tomato & Plum Gazpacho, PAGE 79

Strawberry & Tomato Gazpacho, PAGE 80

Lettuce Gazpacho, PAGE 81

Tomato & Roasted Beet Gazpacho, PAGE 82

White & Green Asparagus Soup, PAGE 83

Watercress Soup, PAGE 84

Zucchini Soup, PAGE 85

Senegalese Soup, British Style, PAGE 86

Smoked Salmon Soup, PAGE 87

HOT SOUPS

Creamy Garlic Soup, PAGE 88

Spanish Onion Soup, PAGE 89

Everyday Vegetable Purée, PAGE 90

Mushroom Soup with Tarragon & Truffle Oil, PAGE 93

Sopa de Picadillo, PAGE 94

Shrimp & Crab Curry Chowder, PAGE 95

MAKING BROTHS, CHOWDERS AND SOUPS ALWAYS GIVES ME THAT FEELING OF GODDESS-LIKE DOMESTICITY. IT MUST BE BECAUSE I THINK

soups are among the most rudimentary and basic of all endeavors in the kitchen. There is something about putting a large pot on the stove, filling it with vegetables, herbs and broth and letting it all simmer together that sustains me, over and over again. Soups are comforting and familiar; they are food for the soul.

I often make soups on Sunday evenings as a way to clean out my refrigerator and begin the week anew. Using slightly wilted vegetables and even their stems and leaves to make a simple broth results in more flavorful soups, eliminating the need for lots of heavy cream or tons of salt. Mushroom, cauliflower, broccoli stems and asparagus spears, in particular, add incredible depth of flavor. It is really not complicated to just boil a little water with a bunch of peppercorns and a bay leaf with things that were going to be thrown out anyway.

Some soups are perfect served cold, others must be served hot and there are those that may be served either way. In the summer months, I always have a batch of cold soup in the refrigerator and eat it most nights when we are not out to dinner. Hot and hearty soups may seem only appropriate in the winter months, but I actually find myself serving them on cool summer evenings, when the sun goes down and the ocean breezes come up. A simple bowl of hot soup finishes the day on a glorious and comforting note. I like making soups heartier by adding generous garnishes like crabmeat, grilled shrimp, mango chutney, dollops of yogurt and croutons.

For a swell dinner party, I add luxurious notes such as grilled lobster or a dollop of caviar. For a midweek dinner, there is nothing as delicious as soup accompanied by a slice of buttered bread, or toasted bread floating in soup with a poached egg on top. It makes for a soothing, nourishing main course.

One of my favorite dinners is a hearty soup like the Shrimp & Crab Curry Chowder, page 95, followed by a green salad and cheese course. I often serve this for dinner parties in Palm Beach during the height of the season when we are all tired of lamb chops and in Southampton during winter months when we can gather around the fireplace for a cozy dinner at home.

I am not a fan of plating hot soups at the beginning of dinner parties. By the time everyone sits down, the soup is at room temperature, or worse, tepid. Invest in one or two soup tureens and pass the soup with a ladle. It's a wise purchase even if you don't serve soup often, because the tureen can double as an elegant centerpiece on its own, filled with greenery or fruits if you like.

Yellow Gazpacho

Gold heirloom tomatoes and yellow peppers make a delicious, sunny summer soup, one that's a bit sweeter than its more common red cousin. I love serving it with salty slivers of fried Serrano ham, and crunchy croutons. No gazpacho is served in Spain without chopped hard-boiled eggs as a garnish. To serve gazpacho, I arrange all the garnishes in small piles on a large platter, then pass it around the table; in Spain there are ceramic dishes made especially for this purpose with separations for each ingredient.

2 pounds yellow tomatoes

½ yellow pepper, chopped

½ yellow onion, chopped

1 clove of garlic

1 cup cucumber, peeled and diced

4 tablespoons white wine vinegar

½ cup olive oil

Sea salt

In a food processor and working in batches, purée all the tomatoes, bell peppers, onion, garlic and cucumber until smooth, at least 5 minutes to aerate the mixture. Strain through a medium sieve into a pitcher and chill until ready to serve. Drizzle the vinegar and olive oil into the soup and season with salt. Taste to adjust seasonings. Arrange the garnishes on a large platter and place on the table. Invite guests to place garnishes in their bowls, then fill with the gazpacho.

SERVES 6

Tomato & Plum Gazpacho

This very simple soup encompasses the flavor of summer. Use red plums and ripe tomatoes. Make it the day before for the flavors to develop and strain it to remove skin and pits. I love it by itself; plain and simple. The combination of plums and tomatoes is so complex and rare it needs nothing else.

6 large ripe tomatoes

6 plums, pitted

½ red onion, chopped

½ cup fresh basil leaves

½ cup olive oil

½ cup red wine vinegar

Sea salt

Combine the tomatoes, plums, onion and basil in a blender and purée until smooth. Add the olive oil and vinegar. Season with salt. Taste to adjust seasonings. Pass the soup through a strainer to remove seeds and skin. Chill until ready to serve.

SERVES 6

Strawberry & Tomato Gazpacho

In the fall, the last of the tomatoes and strawberries are still around in the market. Sweet strawberries add a wonderful dimension to this classic gazpacho. It does need to be strained to remove the seeds, so give yourself enough time to do so. To make this gazpacho light and fluffy, leave the blender running for at least 5 minutes per batch; it will aerate it, giving it a wonderful texture. Arrange croutons, chopped hard-boiled eggs and diced cucumbers on a platter for garnishes.

1 pound ripe tomatoes, diced

1 pound ripe strawberries, hulled and sliced

½ small white onion, diced

½ green bell pepper, membranes removed and diced

½ cup cucumber, peeled and diced

1 clove of garlic

Salt

4 tablespoons olive oil

In a blender or food processor and working in batches, purée the tomatoes, strawberries, onion, pepper, cucumber and garlic until smooth. Strain through a medium sieve into a pitcher and season with salt. Chill in the refrigerator until ready to serve. Drizzle the olive oil into the gazpacho just before serving. Garnish as desired.

SERVES 4

Lettuce Gazpacho

This bright green soup is so delicious it seems impossible it could be good for you, too. The flavor of crisp romaine lettuce is freshness itself and the creamy consistency of yogurt is the perfect base. I also make this soup using other greens like baby spinach, watercress or arugula. Strain it through a medium sieve to make it as smooth as velvet. A sprinkling of fresh herbs as garnish enhances the green palette.

2 heads romaine lettuce

2 cups plain yogurt

1 clove of garlic

½ cup fresh mixed herbs such as parsley, mint and basil

4 tablespoons olive oil

2 tablespoons lemon juice

Salt and pepper to taste

In a blender and working in batches purée the lettuce, yogurt, garlic, herbs, olive oil, and lemon juice until smooth. Add a little water, if necessary, to achieve the consistency of vichyssoise. Strain the soup through a medium sieve into a bowl and chill until ready to serve. Ladle into shallow rimmed soup bowls and garnish with fresh chopped soft herbs.

SERVES 4

Tomato & Roasted Beet Gazpacho

The earthy flavor of beets combined with the acidity of tomatoes makes this simple soup surprisingly complex in flavor. Ladle it into white bowls and add a dollop of sour cream or crème fraîche just before serving for a smart, fresh summer starter. Follow it up with a simple grilled fish as a main course. By the way, in a fit of total madness, I once placed this gazpacho in an ice cream machine and allowed it to churn for about 20 minutes. After freezing it, I scooped it into bowls and served it with crème fraîche and garnished it with edible flowers for a fantastic, delicious and colorful first course.

1 pound fresh beets, about 5 to 6 small ones, trimmed of leaves and washed

2 pounds ripe, red tomatoes, blanched and peeled (see Box, page 133)

1 small onion, diced

4 tablespoons olive oil

Salt and fresh ground pepper

Preheat the oven to 350°F. Place the beets on a cookie sheet and roast until a knife inserted into the thickest part of the beet comes out easily, about 45 minutes. When cool enough to handle, peel and dice.

In a blender and working in batches, purée the beets, tomatoes and onion until smooth. Strain through a medium-size sieve. Add the olive oil, salt and pepper and taste to adjust seasonings. Chill in the refrigerator until ready to serve.

SERVES 6

White & Green Asparagus Soup

Whenever white asparagus appears in the market, I always grab a bunch to make this soup. Of course, when green asparagus is plentiful in the spring, I make this soup all of the time. For an extravagant first course, serve this soup with a drizzle of truffle olive oil. For somewhat fancy dinner parties, I make a batch of each, white and green, and pour them both into a large soup tureen. The colors remain separated until you stir it to serve, making a dazzling presentation. Serve this soup with crunchy, buttery croutons or slivers of crispy Serrano ham.

- 3 pounds green or white asparagus, trimmed, peeled and chopped, stems and peel reserved
- 5 cups Vegetable Stock, page 103
- 2 tablespoons butter
- 2 tablespoons olive oil
- 1 leek, carefully washed and sliced, white part only
- 1 small potato, peeled and diced
- Salt and white pepper
- ½ cup heavy cream

In a large stockpot over medium heat, combine the stock, stems and peels and simmer until very fragrant, about 30 minutes. Strain through a fine sieve and discard the solids. Set aside.

In another stockpot, heat the oil and butter over medium-high heat until foaming. Add the leek and sauté until soft. Add the potato, asparagus spears and 4 cups of the reserved asparagus broth. Season with salt and white pepper. Reduce the heat to low and simmer until the potatoes and the asparagus become tender, about 20 minutes.

Working in batches, purée the soup in a blender until silky; pass through a sieve. Add the heavy cream. Chill in the refrigerator until ready to serve.

SERVES 6

Watercress Soup

I was told that spicy watercress grows on one side of the river while the sweet one we all love grows on the other. Well, I have actually picked watercress from the side of rivers but I was too young to appreciate its flavors until much later in life. When I think back on it, I believe I must have tried the spicy one. At local markets, only sweet watercress is available. It makes a delicious, bright and flavorful soup perfect for year-round entertaining. It lends itself to all manner of garnishes. I love a simple dollop of crème fraîche or sour cream.

1 yellow potato, peeled and diced

1 yellow onion, diced

6 cups Chicken Stock, page 100

½ cup heavy cream

Salt and fresh ground pepper

4 cups fresh watercress, stems removed

In a large stockpot over medium heat, combine the potato, onion, stock and heavy cream. Season generously with salt and pepper. Bring to a boil and simmer until the vegetables are tender, about 15 minutes. Add the watercress and cook until softened, about 3 more minutes. In a blender, working in batches, purée the soup until smooth. Strain into a bowl or pitcher and chill for at least 3 hours. Serve chilled.

SERVES 6

Zucchini Soup

The delicate flavor of zucchini, its versatility, quick growing season and price make it a fantastic year-round ingredient. I adore zucchini grilled, sautéed, fried, steamed and baked. Simply seasoned or extravagantly prepared, zucchini lends itself to all manner of preparation. I often use it in winter months as a filling for vegetable lasagna in place of creamed spinach and as a side dish with fish. In this soup, the onions and the zucchini are sautéed and slightly browned to bring out their depth of flavor, then puréed to the desired consistency. For the children, I add a handful of rice to the zucchini to make it richer and creamier. Serve hot or cold.

- 4 tablespoons olive oil
- 1 yellow onion, sliced
- 2 cloves of garlic, chopped
- 1 tablespoon red pepper flakes
- 4 pounds zucchini, diced
- 4 cups Chicken Stock, page 100
- Salt and fresh ground pepper
- ½ cup fresh basil leaves, chopped

In a large sauté pan, heat the olive oil over medium heat. Add the onions and garlic and sauté until soft and translucent. Add the red pepper flakes and stir. Add the chopped zucchini and stir. Add the chicken stock, raise the heat and bring to a boil. Reduce the heat and simmer until the vegetables are tender, about 20 minutes. Transfer to a blender and purée until smooth. Season with salt and pepper to taste. Chill in the refrigerator until ready to serve. Stir in the basil just before serving.

SERVES 8

Senegalese Soup, British Style

This super-easy curry-based cream soup is delightful year-round. Serve it garnished with diced chicken, grilled shrimp or mango chutney from a jar. Use homemade chicken broth if at all possible; otherwise, choose a very good quality packaged version, preferably organic and low-sodium. Taste the broth before using to insure that it will not overpower the delicate flavors here.

4 tablespoons butter

2 tablespoons curry powder

2 tablespoons flour

1 quart Chicken Stock, page 100

Juice of two lemons

1 cup heavy cream

Salt and white pepper

In a large stockpot over medium-high heat, melt the butter. Add the curry powder and stir to combine. Add the flour and combine well. Add the chicken stock and bring to a boil. Reduce the heat and simmer for a few minutes to thicken. Add the lemon juice and remove from the heat. Cool slightly, stirring occasionally to prevent the mixture from forming a crust. Add the heavy cream. Season with salt and white pepper. Cool and refrigerate. Serve chilled.

SERVES 8 TO 10

Smoked Salmon Soup

My sister Silvia, who is a wonderful cook, gave me this recipe. I have made it regularly ever since, to great reviews. It is rich, creamy and elegant, the perfect beginning for a swell dinner. Serve this followed by a beef tenderloin or roast chicken.

4 tablespoons butter

4 leeks, carefully cleaned and thinly sliced, white part only

2 cloves of garlic, chopped

2 quarts Shellfish Stock, page 102

1 large potato, peeled and diced

½ pound smoked salmon, cut into 1-inch pieces, plus more for garnish

Salt and white pepper

3 cups heavy cream

In a large stockpot over low heat, melt the butter. Add the leeks and garlic and sauté until soft, being careful not to brown them. Add the potatoes and the stock. Simmer for about 20 minutes, until the potato is totally soft. Remove from the heat and let cool until no longer steaming. Add the smoked salmon. Working in batches, purée the mixture in a blender or food processor until smooth (using a blender will result in a finer texture than the food processor). Season to taste with salt and white pepper. Stir in the heavy cream, cool and refrigerate to chill. Before serving, taste to adjust seasonings. Garnish with chopped chives, mango chutney, salmon caviar or additional diced smoked salmon.

SERVES 6

Creamy Garlic Soup

*Do not let the pedestrian ingredients deter you from making this soup; the resulting flavors
are actually quite complex. This cream-based garlic soup makes a wonderful lunch when you
float a piece of fried bread on top, covered with a poached egg. For elegant dinner parties, the
garnishes can be decadent: diced foie gras; or caviar on blini; or pieces of grilled lobster.
Serve it before a rich meat course for a wonderful winter dinner.*

1 head of garlic, peeled

2 quarts Chicken Stock, page 100

1 loaf white country bread, crusts removed and diced

1 cup heavy cream

Salt and fresh ground pepper

In a small pan filled with boiling water, blanch the garlic for a few minutes. Remove with a slotted
spoon and repeat.

In a stockpot, combine the chicken stock and garlic. Bring to a simmer over medium heat. Cook
until the garlic is soft, about 10 minutes. Add the bread and bring to a boil. Add the cream and
stir until heated through. Season with salt and pepper and remove from the heat. In batches,
purée the soup in the blender until smooth. Return to a clean stockpot to keep warm. Serve hot.

SERVES 6 TO 8

Spanish Onion Soup

This soup is sensational for entertaining a crowd. It can be prepared days ahead of time and assembled hours before serving. I have served it as a first course followed by roast chicken and a green salad. On other occasions, I serve it as a hearty one-pot meal. It can be made with a single type of onion or a combination of Vidalia, Spanish and white onions; just give them time to caramelize and sweeten to a deep mahogany color. The tomato sauce is best when homemade and the bread must be a day old if it is going to retain its shape.

4 tablespoons olive oil

4 large onions, thinly sliced on a mandolin

2 cloves of garlic, thinly sliced

½ cup white wine

Salt and fresh ground pepper

1 baguette, thinly sliced

4 cups Tomato Sauce, page 116

1 pound fresh manchego cheese, grated

1 cup aged manchego cheese, grated

4 cups Beef Stock, page 101

In a large sauté pan, heat the olive oil until smoking. Add the onions and garlic and cook until the onions are caramelized and turn a dark golden color, about 20 minutes. Add the white wine and simmer until it nearly evaporates, scraping the bottom of the pan to remove all the drippings. Season with salt and pepper.

Preheat the oven to 350°F. Spoon half of the tomato sauce into an ovenproof dish. Arrange enough bread slices on it to cover the bottom of the dish. Scatter half of the onions over the bread. Top with half of the fresh cheese. Repeat with remaining bread, onions and fresh cheese. Finish with remaining tomato sauce. Scatter the aged manchego on top. Pour the broth into the dish until it reaches the top and let it rest until the bread soaks up the broth, about 20 minutes. Bake until the top is golden and the sauce bubbles, about 30 minutes.

SERVES 6 TO 8

Everyday Vegetable Purée

On Sunday afternoons, when the fridge is full of vegetables from the farmer's market and I am anticipating a very busy week, I often make enough soup to last through the following Friday. It is the perfect quick lunch and the ideal dinner should I arrive home late. What's more, home-made soups keep me from eating the things I should not. The ingredients in my soups vary depending on the season; some weeks they're a purée of carrots and broccoli, or lettuce and potatoes; other times I combine cauliflower and apples. I prefer to limit my vegetable purées to two main ingredients; any more than that and the flavors are clouded. Whatever the pairing, it can sometimes include a roasted vegetable or two, which generally makes a sweeter and more robust soup, whereas sautéed or boiled vegetables results in a purée that is a bit more delicate.

Puréeing the soup in a food processor yields a thicker consistency; the blender makes the soups fine and velvety smooth. For fibrous ingredients that need straining, the blender will yield better results. Always purée in batches and fill the blender or food processor only halfway; the steam rises to the top and can burn you, or explode and make a huge mess in the kitchen. Use an oven mitt or a towel to hold the top in place for extra security.

Less a recipe than a method, the following is designed for improvisation. For example, when my soup is heavy on carrots, I add a little ginger to the onions. To cauliflower, I add pears and to broccoli lots of parsley. These vegetable soups keep in the fridge for a few days and in the freezer for months.

4 tablespoons olive oil

1 small onion, diced

2 cloves of garlic, chopped

½ cup white wine

3 stalks celery, diced

3 pounds total of 1 or 2 vegetables: carrots, broccoli, cauliflower, zucchini

1 small potato, peeled and diced

6 cups Chicken Stock, page 100, or Vegetable Stock, page 103

1 bay leaf

Sea salt and fresh ground pepper

In a stockpot, heat the olive oil over medium-high heat. Add the onions and garlic and sauté until soft and translucent; season lightly with sea salt. Add the white wine and simmer until it evaporates. Add the celery and sauté until soft, 6 to 8 minutes. Stir in the vegetables, cooking about 5 minutes. Add the stock and bay leaf. Season with pepper. Raise the heat to high and bring to a boil. Reduce the heat to medium and simmer until the vegetables are very soft, about 30 minutes. Remove and discard the bay leaf.

Working in batches, purée the soup in a blender or food processor until very fine. Pass it through a strainer if needed and return it to a clean pot to keep warm until ready to serve.

SERVES 6

Mushroom Soup with Tarragon & Truffle Oil

What this soup lacks in looks it makes up in taste. Lots of fresh tarragon and a drizzle (or two) of truffle oil is all it takes to make it sensational. I use one kind or a mixture of mushrooms like Portobello, shiitake, chanterelle and oyster.

2 pounds whole mushrooms, mixed or single variety, brushed clean and trimmed, stems reserved

4 tablespoons olive oil

2 cups fresh tarragon leaves, plus more sprigs for garnish

5 cloves of garlic

1 medium yellow onion, diced

4 celery stalks, diced

Sea salt and fresh ground pepper

½ cup heavy cream

½ cup Parmesan

1 tablespoon black truffle oil (or more to taste)

To make the stock, heat 1 tablespoon oil over medium heat in a large stockpot. Add the stems and sauté until brown, about 5 minutes. Add 1 clove of garlic, 1 cup tarragon leaves and sauté until fragrant, about 2 minutes. Add 8 cups of water and bring to a boil. Lower the heat and simmer to reduce the liquid to 6 cups, about 20 minutes. Strain the broth through a fine sieve and reserve; discard the solids.

In a clean stockpot, heat the remaining olive oil over medium heat. Add the remaining garlic, onions and celery and sauté until soft. Add the mushrooms and season generously with salt and pepper and sauté until soft. Add the reserved mushroom stock and tarragon leaves and bring to a boil. Then simmer until the mushrooms are tender; about 15 minutes.

Working in batches, purée the soup in a blender and return to the pot to serve warm. Serve with fresh pepper and sliced mushrooms.

SERVES 6

Sopa de Picadillo

This classic Andalucian soup is my family's version of chicken soup. We used to have it as children when we were not feeling well and also during Lent as a light supper. Be sure to use an excellent quality broth if you are not making your own. At elegant dinner parties I serve this soup in delicate consommé cups.

- 6 cups Beef Stock, page 101
- 4 ounces Serrano or Virginia ham, finely chopped
- 1 breast of chicken, poached and finely diced
- 3 hard-boiled eggs, finely chopped
- ½ cup dry fino sherry
- 2 tablespoons chopped fresh mint

Pour the broth into a large stockpot and bring to a boil over high heat. Reduce the heat to medium and add the ham, chicken, hard-boiled eggs, sherry and mint leaves and simmer until heated through, about 10 minutes. Ladle into consommé cups and serve.

SERVES 4

Shrimp & Crab Curry Chowder

This is a total crowd pleaser. I serve it with fluffy white rice and lots of garnishes, sort of like you would serve chili. Favorites are diced tomatoes, chopped scallions, mango chutney, coconut shaves and toasted pine nuts.

3 tablespoons olive oil

1 large yellow onion, diced

2 cloves of garlic, chopped

1 tablespoon chili powder

1 tablespoon turmeric

1 tablespoon curry powder

1 tablespoon coriander

1 yellow pepper, membrane removed and diced

1 pound white corn kernels, fresh or frozen

1 cup Chicken Stock, page 100

1 cup coconut milk

1 pound shrimp, cleaned

1 pound crabmeat, picked over

Salt and fresh ground pepper

In a large stockpot, heat the olive oil over medium-high heat. Add the onion and garlic and sauté until transparent. Add the chili powder, turmeric and curry and stir to coat well with the oil until fragrant. Add the pepper and sauté until bright, about 3 minutes. Add the corn and chicken stock, stirring between each addition. Bring to a boil, reduce the heat and simmer for about 10 minutes. Add the coconut milk and shrimp. Raise the heat and return to a boil. Simmer for 5 to 8 minutes, until the shrimp turn pink. Add the crabmeat, heat through and season with salt and pepper. Serve hot.

SERVES 8 TO 10

Sauces

Chicken Stock, PAGE 100

Beef Stock, PAGE 101

Shellfish Stock, PAGE 102

Vegetable Stock, PAGE 103

Preserved Lemons, PAGE 105

Homemade Mayonnaise, PAGE 106

Aïoli (Alioli), PAGE 107

Mustard & Lemon Mayonnaise, PAGE 107

Mayonnaise with Truffle Oil, PAGE 107

Mayonnaise with Mint, PAGE 108

Eggless Mayonnaise, PAGE 108

Curry Mayonnaise "Al Fresco," PAGE 109

Salsa Andaluza (Pink Mayonnaise), PAGE 109

Pink Béchamel Sauce, PAGE 110

Salsa Española, PAGE 111

Mushroom Cream Sauce, British Style, PAGE 112

Fresh Herb Sauce & Marinade, PAGE 113

Roasted Garlic Dip & Marinade, PAGE 115

Tomato Sauce (Salsa de Tomate), PAGE 116

Tomato Jam, Moroccan Style, PAGE 117

SAUCES, STOCKS AND MARINADES TRANSFORM BASIC INGREDIENTS AND INFUSE THEM WITH FLAVOR

and taste. Having a repertoire of these has saved me from many potential culinary disasters. The simple act of blending a few ingredients together to give a burst of flavor to a dish is the difference between one that is just edible to one that becomes sublime.

Sauces, marinades and broths have become the backbone of my recipe collection. For all of their flavor benefits they also add charm to mundane ingredients, and, depending on how you use them, transform a bland dish into one that is deliciously elegant. A simple piece of grilled beef or tender lamb chop marinated in a simple mix of fresh herbs and olive oil transforms them. The Tomato Sauce, page 116, makes for a knockout meatloaf, adding extra richness from the caramelized tomatoes. This is a basic sauce for many Mediterranean dishes and one that is easily mastered. Make it to suit your tastes; experiment with different herbs to bring out their unique flavor.

Roasted Garlic & Rosemary Spread is a boon to a fresh piece of grilled fish — it's all you need to dress it up. And Salsa Española, page 111, made with caramelized carrots and onions, is delicious with anything from meatballs to chicken.

Despite what you may think, making stocks from scratch is easy when you do it while cooking other dishes. They require a little bit of chopping, filling up a pot with water, and heat. That's it. They need very little attention from the cook as they quietly simmer in a big pot on the stove. The goodness and flavor they give food is unparalleled. You can tweak them to fit your taste and the dish you are making and, thus, they achieve the depth of flavor associated with haute cuisine. Always make more than you need and freeze the excess, so that you'll have it on hand the next time you need it. If making your own stock is not doable, purchase the organic kind, preferably low-sodium, and enhance it with some fresh ingredients to bring out its flavor.

I have separated the stocks into beef, chicken and shellfish but I have to admit I have mixed beef and chicken ingredients to make a sensational all-purpose broth that is great with everything. Do freeze them in one- or two-cup containers or in plastic bags for easy defrosting.

Once you discover the versatility, utility and, above all, the deep flavor sauces, stocks and marinades from this chapter bring to dishes, you will make them over and over — and eventually commit them to your culinary memory as I have.

Chicken Stock

Keep a plastic bag with cooked chicken carcasses (the ones from successful roast chickens or Thanksgiving turkey) in the freezer and make this broth when you have 2 or 3. Use any vegetables that you have in the bottom of the fridge but avoid broccoli and potatoes, as they will cloud the broth. Once it is made, cool the broth, then freeze it in one- or two-cup containers for easy defrosting.

2 onions, skin on, roughly chopped

1 leek, cleaned and sliced

1 turnip, peeled and roughly chopped

4 carrots, chopped

4 stalks celery, chopped

2 cooked chicken carcasses

1 sprig marjoram

1 sprig thyme

1 sprig rosemary

4 fresh bay leaves

10 peppercorns

Put all the ingredients in an 8-quart pot and add enough water to cover the chicken bones. Bring to a boil, reduce the heat and simmer over low heat for 2 to 3 hours, adding more water if it falls below the bones. While the stock simmers, remove the foam that collects on the surface with a spoon. Strain the stock through a sieve. Strain a second time through a finer mesh sieve, kitchen towel or muslin cloth. Pour into containers to cool, removing the fat that rises to the top. Store, covered, in the refrigerator for two days, or freeze up to 2 months.

MAKES 8 CUPS

Beef Stock

For this stock, I use bones from hams, veal and beef. Mix it all for a rich and flavorful broth to use for making risottos, soups and sauces. Throw in the skins of the onions as that gives the broth a wonderful golden color. As with the chicken stock, any vegetables aside from broccoli and potato will lend this stock fine flavor.

2 onions, skin on, roughly chopped

1 leek, washed and chopped

1 turnip, peeled and chopped

4 carrots, peeled and chopped

1 cup mushroom stems, chopped

4 stalks celery, chopped

1 pound mix of veal, beef or pork bones

2 tablespoons tomato paste

4 cloves of garlic, peeled

8 stems parsley

8 black peppercorns

Put all ingredients in an 8-quart pot and add enough water to cover the bones. Bring to a boil, reduce the heat to low and simmer for 2 to 3 hours. Once in a while, remove the foam with a spoon. Simmer for at least two hours; three is better, adding more water if it falls below the bones. Strain through a fine mesh sieve, kitchen towel or muslin cloth. Pour into containers to cool, removing the fat that rises to the top. Store, covered, in the refrigerator for two days, or freeze up to 2 months.

MAKES 8 CUPS

Shellfish Stock

If you can find head-on shrimp, save the heads in a plastic bag in the freezer until you have about 2 dozen. Lobster heads and carcasses make a flavorful broth, too. This shellfish broth is sensational as the base for any risotto, paella or rice dish that features fish. Simmer the broth for about 20 minutes until it becomes pink; any longer and it will become bitter.

2 pounds mixed seafood shells, such as shrimp and lobster

1 onion, peel on, quartered

10 whole peppercorns

1 lemon, halved

1 bay leaf

In an 8-quart stockpot, combine the shrimp and/or lobster shells, onion, peppercorns, bay leaf and the lemon. Fill with cold water to cover the ingredients by at least 1 inch and bring to a boil. Reduce the heat to low and simmer for about 20 minutes. Strain the stock through a fine mesh strainer or tea towel. Pour into 1-cup containers to cool. Cover and refrigerate up to 2 days or freeze up to 1 month.

MAKES 8 CUPS

Vegetable Stock

This light broth is essential for making delicate soups and sauces. Asparagus ends, broccoli stems, cauliflowers, carrots, shells of peas and mushrooms stems all make a sensational broth. Also use leeks, scallions, turnips and artichokes. Refrain from using potatoes and broccoli florets as they will cloud the broth.

When I don't have time to make vegetable broth from scratch, I often use a good organic store-bought brand and enhance it with whatever vegetables I have in the fridge. Simmering the broth for 20 to 30 minutes is all it takes to imbue the liquid with great flavor.

2 pounds of any combination of vegetable ends or stems such as mushrooms, asparagus and broccoli stems, washed and trimmed

1 onion

10 peppercorns

1 bay leaf

In an 8-quart stockpot, combine the vegetables, onion and peppercorns. Fill with cold water to cover and bring to a boil. Add the bay leaf. Reduce the heat and simmer for about 20 minutes. Strain through a fine mesh sieve, kitchen towel or muslin cloth. Pour into containers to cool. Store, covered, in the refrigerator for two days, or freeze up to 6 months.

MAKES 8 CUPS

Preserved Lemons

A staple in the Moroccan pantry, preserved lemons infuse chicken dishes and roasts with unique, sensational flavor. In the true way of preserving lemons, it takes a full month for them to marinate in a jar. This version is a bit quicker—it takes just 5 days—as the lemons are cooked in generously salted water and then marinated. I make a batch at the beginning of the summer and use it throughout the warm months, when I entertain at home quite often.

12 organic lemons (if not organic, clean them to remove any wax coating)

2 cups coarse sea salt

4 cinnamon sticks

1 tablespoon coriander seeds

1 tablespoon whole cumin seeds

1 tablespoon black peppercorns

1 teaspoon cloves

5 fresh bay leaves

Olive oil

In a 4-quart stockpot filled with water, combine the lemons, salt, cinnamon, coriander, cumin, peppercorns, cloves and bay leaves. Bring to a boil and continue to boil until the lemons turn soft, about 45 minutes. Transfer the lemons with their cooking liquid and spices to several large Mason jars, cover, and leave to cure at room temperature 5 days.

After five days, remove the lemons from the curing liquid and rinse thoroughly. Slice in half, scoop out the pulp and discard. Coarsely chop the rind. Place the rinds in a clean jar and add olive oil to cover. Cover and store in the refrigerator. Bring to room temperature before using.

MAKES 1 1/2 CUPS

Homemade Mayonnaise

Spaniards claim the invention of mayonnaise in the 1700s on the island of Mahon, in the Balearic Islands. There are some reports of a French cook involved, but it was on Spanish soil so I am claiming it for Spain! I make it in the blender and play with thickness and flavors depending on what I am serving. When I am making it to accompany fish dishes, I add a bit more lemon; for potatoes and vegetables, an extra dash of vinegar brightens it and a tablespoon of curry mixed in makes a perfect dressing for shrimp. The proportions of egg and olive oil are always the same; the amount of additional flavoring you use is up to you. Herbs can make a dramatic difference in a mayonnaise; my favorites are tarragon, rosemary and oregano. Be careful not to add too much oregano, though; the flavor is really intense and it can overpower the rest of the ingredients. Taste the mayonnaise as you make it; you can always add more flavor as you go along.

1 large egg

1 large egg yolk

2 tablespoons lemon juice

2 tablespoons white wine vinegar

Pinch of salt

1 cup olive oil

Place egg, yolk, lemon juice, vinegar and salt in the blender. Purée until smooth. With the motor running, pour the olive oil in a stream until the mixture is emulsified and thick. Cover and chill until ready to serve. The mayonnaise will keep, covered, in the refrigerator up to 2 days.

MAKES 1 1/2 CUPS

Aïoli (Alioli)

This mayonnaise, infused with garlic for a pungent and flavorful kick, is the perfect way to enhance soups, seafood dishes and —my favorite— paella. Make it in the morning and let it chill in the fridge so the flavors develop. Always taste as you go along to adjust the flavors to your taste. Because it is made with raw eggs, I serve it straight from the fridge. Aïoli is a versatile recipe, as simple or as special as you'd like to make it. In Provençe and Cataluna, this lively mayonnaise transforms basic steamed vegetables into the aptly named Le Grand Aïoli.

To make, add 2 cloves of garlic to the blender and continue as in Homemade Mayonnaise, page 106.

MAKES 1 1/2 CUPS

Mustard & Lemon Mayonnaise

This is my go-to dip for steamed prawns, boiled potatoes and steamed vegetables.

To make, add 1 tablespoon of country-style mustard to Homemade Mayonnaise, page 106.

MAKES 1 1/2 CUPS

Mayonnaise with Truffle Oil

What could be more decadent than dipping freshly made French fries into a bowl of mayonnaise made with truffle oil? Not much! Make this mayonnaise to give a fabulous kick to sausages grilled in white wine, steaks or simply grilled mushrooms. The flavor is very intense and it does need to rest. Use good quality truffle oil and a mild-flavored olive oil to excite your taste buds, not drive them crazy!

To make, add 1 tablespoon of black or white truffle oil to Homemade Mayonnaise.

MAKES 1 1/2 CUPS

Mayonnaise with Mint

I adore this bright green mayonnaise not only for the taste, but because it brightens up anything you put it on, whether it is white fish, sliced tomatoes or creamy risotto. Add a dollop to steamed vegetables or on the side of sautéed shrimp. Chopped mint leaves and cider vinegar make this tangy sauce a perfect dressing for fresh tomatoes or as an accompaniment for cold lamb.

To make, puree a cup of fresh mint leaves in the blender and continue as in Homemade Mayonnaise, page 106.

MAKES 1 1/2 CUPS

Eggless Mayonnaise

This milk-based, eggless mayonnaise is a great solution for those on restrictive diets, the very young, and the elderly, who should not eat raw eggs. You can add any of the ingredients mentioned here to make your own flavors. Use a mild olive oil that won't compete with the flavor of the milk. This is a thinner sauce, perfect as salad dressing.

½ cup milk

1 tablespoon lemon juice

1 tablespoon Dijon mustard

Pinch of salt

1 cup olive oil

In a blender, combine the milk, lemon juice, mustard and salt. Purée until blended. With the motor running, pour the olive oil in a stream until thick and emulsified. Cover and chill until ready to serve. The mayonnaise will keep, covered, in the refrigerator up to 2 days. Chill until ready to use.

MAKES 1 CUP

Curry Mayonnaise "Al Fresco"

Rather than using my Homemade Mayonnaise to make this flavorful dressing, I prefer to use the purchased kind since I use it to make Layered Curried Chicken Salad, page 130, a dish I make often in the summertime, when we typically eat outdoors. It can withstand the heat a bit longer than mayonnaise made with raw eggs.

2 cups purchased mayonnaise

1 cup sour cream

½ cup milk

1 teaspoon chili powder

3 tablespoons curry powder

1 pinch of salt

In a bowl, combine the mayonnaise, sour cream, milk, chili powder, curry and salt. Whisk together until well-combined. Cover and chill in the refrigerator up to 3 days.

MAKES 3 ½ CUPS

Salsa Andaluza (Pink Mayonnaise)

Fresh tomatoes and roasted red peppers gives this sauce its pretty light pink color. Use it to dress potatoes, tomatoes and egg salad. It's also a great dip for crudités, crab cakes and for spreading on sandwiches.

To make, add to the blender 1 peeled tomato (see Box, page 133) and 1 roasted red pepper and continue as in Homemade Mayonnaise, page 106.

MAKES 2 CUPS

Pink Béchamel Sauce

This deliciously velvet sauce is ideal to serve over a stack of Three Vegetable Tortillas, page 143. It is also delicious served with a plain omelet for a Sunday brunch.

2 tablespoons butter

2 tablespoons flour

1 ½ cups milk

2 tablespoons tomato paste or fine tomato purée

Salt and fresh ground pepper

In a saucepan, melt the butter over medium heat. Do not let it brown. Whisk in the flour until blended. Add the milk and, stirring constantly, simmer until the sauce thickens. Add the tomato paste and stir until the sauce is uniform in color. Season to taste with salt and pepper.

MAKES 2 CUPS

Salsa Española

Rich and versatile, Salsa Española has deep flavors from the sweetness of the onion and carrots. I use it as the sauce for meatballs, to serve alongside beef roasts and as a flavorful accompaniment to roast chicken. It is also delicious when layered with steamed, sliced potatoes and then re-baked as in a classic scalloped potatoes dish. I always double this recipe since Salsa Española freezes beautifully.

4 tablespoons olive oil

2 large onions, diced

4 medium carrots, peeled and diced

2 tablespoons all-purpose flour

2 cups Beef Stock, page 101

1 cup fino sherry or very dry white wine

Sea salt and fresh ground pepper

In a large saucepan, heat the olive oil over high heat. Add the onions and sauté until golden brown, about 10 minutes. Add the carrots and flour and stir until the flour dissolves into the mixture. Add the broth and sherry and season with salt and pepper. Bring the sauce to a boil, reduce the heat and simmer until the sauce thickens, about 10 minutes. Working in batches, purée the sauce in a blender or food processor until smooth. Taste to adjust seasonings and return to a clean pot to warm up before serving. The sauce will keep, covered, in the refrigerator up to 5 days or up to 2 months in the freezer.

MAKES 2 CUPS

Mushroom Cream Sauce, British Style

This sauce is one of my earliest achievements in the kitchen. In fact, I learned to make it while in school in England, thus the name. It is the fresh, homemade equivalent to that pantry panacea, canned Mushroom Soup. I use it to fill pastry shells for hors d'oeuvres, to top poached eggs on toast, and as a delicious sauce for tenderloin. I also serve it over pasta for a children-friendly dinner. To make it even more decadent, add a few drops of truffle oil.

- 4 tablespoons butter
- 2 tablespoons olive oil
- 2 pounds white mushrooms, cleaned and roughly chopped
- ½ cup white wine
- 2 tablespoons flour
- 1 pint heavy cream

Place a medium pan over high heat. When it is hot, add the butter and olive oil and heat until hot but not smoking. Add the mushrooms, reduce the heat, and simmer until all the mushroom's liquid is released, about 15 minutes. Add the white wine and simmer until reduced. Add the flour and stir to dissolve the flour. Raise the heat, add the heavy cream and, stirring constantly, bring to a boil. Reduce the heat and simmer until thickened, about 5 to 8 minutes. Use the sauce hot or warm. The sauce will keep, covered in the refrigerator, up to 3 days.

MAKES 6 CUPS

Fresh Herb Sauce & Marinade

I have small herb gardens bursting with mint, basil, parsley, tarragon and sage. Having an abundant supply of herbs gives me the luxury of cooking with all them whenever the inspiration strikes. I make sauces and dressings with some or a mixture of many. Fresh herbs are a must when cooking Mediterranean-style food; freshness and flavors combine to create spectacular dishes. Sometimes I use just one herb, garlic, a little vinegar or lemon juice and olive oil to combine it all. Other times, I mix mint with rosemary or sage and tarragon or even when the batch is a little thin, a mixture of all. I like to experiment with combinations and different varieties. Add more or less olive oil depending on its use. When I use it as a marinade, I like it a little thinner so it spreads easier; when used as a dip, thicker is better.

This sauce works as a marinade, as a dip or just as a sauce for grilled lamb, vegetables, rice and even fish. It is bright green, fresh tasting and infuses great flavor and taste to almost anything. I adore it over just boiled baby potatoes and spooned over roasted vegetables. To me, this fresh herb sauce is like music on my plate.

1 cup mixed fresh herbs such as sage, parsley, mint, tarragon or chives

1 clove of garlic

½ cup olive oil

Juice of 1 lemon

Pinch of salt

Combine the herbs, garlic, olive oil, lemon and salt in a blender and purée until smooth. Serve and use at room temperature. The sauce will keep, covered, in the refrigerator up to 3 days.

MAKES 1 CUP

Roasted Garlic Dip & Marinade

When roasted, garlic becomes sweet, caramelized and creamy. Add a good-quality olive oil and fresh rosemary and you are instantly transported to Provençe. I serve this dip with something as simple as a fresh baguette, use it to sauté vegetables and swirl it into soups. It is a great dressing to brush on steaks and lamb chops just before grilling and makes a healthy alternative to sour cream on baked potatoes. I always make this dip when girls come to my kitchen lunches and sit around while I cook. Eaten with a fresh, warm baguette while sipping cool white wine is my idea of perfect.

- 3 heads garlic, about 1 cup, peeled
- 2 rosemary sprigs, needles removed and roughly chopped
- 10 peppercorns
- ½ cup best-quality extra-virgin olive oil

Turn the oven to 300°F. Spread the garlic cloves on a parchment-lined cookie sheet. Cover with tin foil. Bake 15-20 minutes. The cloves should maintain their shape but turn golden and will be soft to the touch. Remove the cloves carefully so as not to break them and place them in a small bowl. Cover with the olive oil, peppercorns and roughly chopped rosemary. Give them a good stir and set aside to cool. The dip will keep, covered, in the refrigerator up to three days. Serve at room temperature.

MAKES ABOUT 1 CUP

Tomato Sauce (Salsa de Tomate)

The most versatile and practical of all the basic sauces shows up in an endless array of Mediterranean dishes. It keeps very well in the fridge, freezes beautifully and never loses its flavor or color.

2 tablespoons olive oil

1 yellow onion, diced

2 cloves of garlic, diced

½ cup dry white wine

Salt and fresh ground pepper

2 16-ounce can diced tomatoes

1 8-ounce can tomato purée

1 tablespoon sugar

1 bay leaf

2 sprigs rosemary, stems removed

In a large sauté pan, heat the olive oil over high heat. Add the onions and garlic and sauté until the onions become translucent. Add the white wine, reduce the heat and simmer until the wine evaporates. Season with the salt and pepper. Add the tomatoes and their juices, the sugar, bay leaf and rosemary. Simmer over low heat until the liquid evaporates and the sauce becomes thick and caramelized, about 1 hour. During the simmering time, stir the sauce once in a while but let it fall to the bottom so it caramelizes.

Store, covered, in the refrigerator for up to 1 week. Remove the bay leaf before serving.

MAKES 5 TO 6 CUPS

Tomato Jam, Moroccan Style

Spices that are standard in the Moroccan pantry imbue this jam with warmth and heat. Cinnamon and chili powder, classic spices of North African cuisine, combine with classic Andalucian ingredients for a uniquely flavored condiment. Spread it on toast or serve alongside cheese and pâté. Sometimes I add a dollop into cream soups.

4 pounds large ripe tomatoes, peeled (see Box, page 133), seeded and diced

2 tablespoons butter

2 tablespoons olive oil

4 cloves of garlic, sliced

1 teaspoon ground cinnamon

1 teaspoon chili powder

3 tablespoons sugar

Sea salt and fresh ground pepper

In a large stockpot, melt the butter and olive oil over high heat until foamy. Add the garlic and cinnamon and sauté until the garlic turns slightly golden. Add the tomatoes and sugar and stir well. Reduce the heat and simmer until the liquid evaporates and the tomatoes caramelize, about 40 minutes. Remove from heat and pour into a clean Mason jar. Cool, uncovered. Cover and refrigerate until chilled. The jam will keep, refrigerated, up to 10 days.

MAKES 4 CUPS

Salads

Zucchini & Blue Cheese Salad, PAGE 122

Orange & Red Onion Salad, PAGE 123

Poached Egg Salad with Red Wine Sauce, PAGE 124

Red Wine Sauce, PAGE 125

Red Pepper & Red Onion Salad, PAGE 126

Romaine Hearts with Crispy Garlic, PAGE 129

Layered Curried Chicken Salad, PAGE 130

Tomato Salad, PAGE 132

Duck Magret & Warm Onion Salad, PAGE 134

Ana Arias' Little Bits Salad, PAGE 135

Prawn & Potato Salad with Warm Mustard Sauce, PAGE 136

Ensaladilla Rusa (Russian Salad), PAGE 137

ENTERTAINING AT LUNCHTIME CALLS FOR LIGHT AND FLAVORFUL DISHES AND NO CHOICE COULD BE BETTER THAN FRESH SALADS.

Some of my recipes are quick and easy for an impromptu lunch and others must be prepared ahead of time. Some are hearty enough to serve as family lunches and others are just perfect when the ladies come for a quick bite.

Here in the States, there is a certain old-world pleasure in relaxing with friends and family midday, but there is also something ideally American about building a meal around a big, healthy salad. I do like one of the courses to be warm or at room temperature and really, only the ice cream comes straight from the freezer. Whether it is an old wives' tale or not, I do believe eating anything that might give you a brain freeze just can't be good for you. Regardless, eating salad that's too cool dulls its flavor. I adore warm salads as they offer the best of both worlds: the goodness of vegetables and the flavor of lightly cooked meats or fish. Shellfish, poultry and eggs are ideal in salads, as they can be paired with almost any sauce or dressing, from creamy to garlicky and even sweet or spicy. Whatever the combination, keep the menu to a one-course hot or cold salad for midweek lunches and avoid too much dairy, heavy meats and sauces, which can leave your guests in a somnolent state. Save these additions for long weekend lunches when taking a well-deserved nap is part of the plan.

Seasonal vegetables are, of course, always best and during the summer months typically Mediterranean vegetables are at their peak of flavor. Local farms, wherever you may live, offer the best produce — just-picked and ripened on the bush, branch or vine, as Mother Nature intended. I like the salads here best when I can get my produce fresh from the farm stand. Though I don't have an orchard in my life now, merely an oversize herb garden, I still like to instill in my children the knowledge of the seasons, of food from the earth and waiting for ripeness and flavor.

Salads that need last-minute assembly are perfect for impromptu lunches; the ones made ahead of time are ideal for larger groups. For picnics or for traveling, choose those that contain no mayonnaise or egg-based sauces, since they can spoil in the heat. Whatever the occasion, always toss salads well. I prefer using oversize bowls or shallow platters, which makes it easy to coat every ingredient evenly with dressing. But use a light hand when dressing any salad! If ever in doubt, err on the side of under-dressing and pass extra with the salad. When entertaining, a beautiful presentation is key. Even the simplest salads can be made elegant and sophisticated with creative plating and artful garnishes.

What to drink with these salads? For summer lunches, serve well-chilled rosé in pretty decanters; rattan-wrapped for eating outside and fine crystal in the dining room. For warm-weather lunches, try a light, fruity rosé or a nice dry white wine. Heartier white wines are lovely for midday winter meals and reds taste just right when the afternoon quickly turns to dusk. And, of course, you can never go wrong with a tall glass of iced tea.

Zucchini & Blue Cheese Salad

Like most amateur gardeners, I find myself with an overabundance of zucchini at summer's end. As a result, I spend an inordinate amount of time coming up with recipes for using it all. This is one of my favorite ways to prepare it, because it's easy to make, delicious and beautiful on the table. To prepare the zucchini, I use a hand-held peeler with small ridges that produce thin strands of zucchini. A mandolin or even a food processor fitted with the julienne blade also works very well. If making this salad ahead of time, prepare all of the ingredients but leave the steaming of the zucchini for the last minute.

½ cup soft blue cheese, crumbled

1 cup plain whole-milk yogurt

2 tablespoons olive oil

1 tablespoon red wine or sherry vinegar

2 tablespoons parsley, finely chopped, plus more for garnish

4 medium zucchini

2 endives

2 large red tomatoes, peeled and diced (see Box, page 133)

Salt and fresh ground pepper

In a small bowl, whisk together the blue cheese, yogurt, olive oil, vinegar and parsley. Season with salt and pepper. The dressing should be the consistency of purchased mayonnaise. Cover and refrigerate for about one hour to allow the flavors to come together.

Bring a medium saucepan filled with salted water to a boil. Meanwhile, line a dinner plate with paper towels. Julienne the zucchini lengthwise. Working in batches, blanch the zucchini in the boiling water until fork-tender, about 3 minutes. Using a slotted spoon, remove the zucchini to the plate to drain. To serve, arrange the endive leaves like the petals of a flower around the edge of a large, rimmed shallow bowl. Pile the zucchini in the center. Scatter the diced tomatoes over the zucchini and drizzle the blue cheese sauce all over. Sprinkle with the remaining parsley and serve.

SERVES 4 TO 6

Orange & Red Onion Salad

This combination of flavors is typical of the Valencia region, famous for its thin-skinned oranges and sweet red onions. Oranges, sliced into slender rounds and paired with red onions cut the same way or chopped, make for a beautiful presentation on a large platter. I like to scatter tiny mint leaves for garnish, but practically any soft herb will enhance its look and flavor. Use oranges and onions of similar size to make the presentation even prettier.

4 large Valencia oranges

1 medium red onion, thinly sliced or chopped

Juice of 1 lemon

½ cup olive oil

Pinch of salt

Pinch of sugar

1 pound baby spinach leaves, washed and dried

1 cup Spiced Walnuts, page 73

Mint leaves for garnish

Peel the oranges over a bowl to collect all of the juices, removing the seeds and as much pith as possible. Cut the orange in crosswise slices, as thinly as possible. In a small bowl, whisk together the collected juices, lemon juice, olive oil, salt and sugar until combined. On a large platter, arrange the spinach leaves in a bed, top with the orange slices, overlapping them.

Arrange the onions on top of the orange slices. Drizzle with the dressing, scatter the walnuts on top and garnish with mint leaves.

SERVES 6

Poached Egg Salad with Red Wine Sauce

Inspired by the classic French salad of frisée and liver, this luscious salad is an elegant lunch offering. I make it for my husband and his business associates when they come for lunch; it gives me the best excuse to hide in the kitchen and let them talk in the other room!

1 pound bacon or lardoons, diced

1 pound mixed mushrooms such as portobello, shiitake and button, bite-sized

½ small onion, thinly sliced

1 cup Red Wine Sauce, page 125

4 cups frisée, romaine and/or watercress, washed, dried and cut into bite-size pieces

4 tablespoons olive oil

4 tablespoons balsamic vinegar

1 small baguette, sliced into 6 1-inch-thick slices, toasted

6 large eggs

Sea salt and fresh ground pepper

In a frying pan over high heat, fry the bacon until crispy. Remove with a slotted spoon or tongs and drain on paper towels. Turn the heat to medium-low, add the mushrooms to the pan, and sauté until they release their liquid and soften, about 8 minutes. Stir in the onions. Add the Red Wine Sauce, bring to a simmer and cook until the onions become soft and slightly tinted with the red wine, 10-15 minutes.

In a large serving bowl, combine the lettuces. In a small bowl, whisk together the oil and vinegar and toss with the lettuces. Using an egg poacher, poach the eggs for 4 minutes and place on top of the toasted baguettes.

To serve, arrange the dressed lettuces on a shallow serving platter. Place the warm poached eggs and baguettes on top. Spoon the mushroom sauce on top of the eggs and scatter the bacon bits all over. Serve immediately.

SERVES 6 AS A FIRST COURSE, DOUBLE THE RECIPE TO SERVE 6 FOR A MAIN COURSE

Red Wine Sauce

This sauce is robust, yet light and flavorful. Serve it with Poached Egg Salad, page 124, or alongside cooked steak or lamb. Yum. It keeps in the refrigerator for a few days, so double the recipe; you'll thank me.

1 cup red wine

½ small onion, diced

1 cup Beef Stock, page 101

8 tablespoons (1 stick) butter, cut into pieces

Sea salt and fresh ground pepper

In a medium saucepan, combine the red wine and onion. Simmer over medium-low heat until reduced by half, about 20 minutes. Add the broth and simmer another 20 minutes over low heat. Incorporate the butter, one piece at a time, whisking with each addition. Remove from the heat and season with salt and pepper. Cover to keep warm until ready to use.

MAKES 1 CUP

Red Pepper & Red Onion Salad

This easy-to-make combination is an excellent side dish to grilled meats or fish. Make it ahead so the flavors develop and the juices meld. Fresh bread to mop up juices is all you need to make this a delicious meal.

6 good quality jarred roasted red peppers drained and sliced;
   reserve 4 tablespoons of liquid or roast them yourself (see Box below)

1 medium red onion, thinly sliced

1 clove of garlic

1 teaspoon sea salt

⅓ cup olive oil

2 tablespoons red wine vinegar

Place the peppers in a shallow serving bowl. Scatter the red onions on top. Using a mortar and pestle or working on a cutting board, mash the garlic with the salt. Slowly whisk in the olive oil in a stream to form a paste. Whisk in the vinegar. Whisk in the reserved red pepper juice. Pour the dressing over the red pepper-onion mixture. Cover tightly and refrigerate until ready to serve.

SERVES 6 TO 8

HOW TO ROAST PEPPERS

Preheat the oven to 450°F. Brush the peppers all over with olive oil and roast for about 20 minutes, turning once. Place them in a paper bag or covered bowl and allow the steam to separate the skin from the flesh. When cool enough to handle, peel and seed, reserving the juices if needed.

Romaine Hearts with Crispy Garlic

Crispy golden garlic is one of my favorite garnishes. I sprinkle it on top of sautéed spinach and diced tomatoes, and use it as a garnish on fried eggs and as a surprising addition to pork tenderloin sandwiches. This salad features few ingredients, but the combination of crunchy, golden garlic, the olive oil that crisps it, and a bit of salt are all you need to enliven the romaine hearts. Keep the hearts intact; arrange them on a shallow platter, then pour the crispy garlic and olive oil over them, just before serving so that the leaves don't wilt. You can always add ingredients to the salad - bacon bits, crumbled blue cheese and cooked jamón Serrano are nice choices–but the truth is, I adore this simple version most.

- 4 tablespoons olive oil
- 1 head garlic, peeled and thinly sliced
- 4 small heads romaine lettuce, white and pale green parts only
- Sea salt

Arrange the romaine hearts on a shallow platter. In a small saucepan, heat the olive oil over medium-high heat. Add the garlic and sauté until pale golden. Using a slotted spoon, remove the garlic from the oil and scatter over the lettuce. Drizzle a bit of oil over the leaves, but not so heavily as to wilt the greens. Season with salt and serve.

SERVES 6 TO 8

Layered Curried Chicken Salad

Layered salads are wonderful choices for luncheons since most of them are best prepared ahead of time to allow the flavors to develop. What makes this curry salad extra special are the matchstick potatoes. They're best fried just before serving, but if this is impossible, fry them no more than one hour before serving and keep them in a medium-hot oven so they remain crispy and warm. For a fantastic summer lunch, serve the salad after a chilled soup such as Strawberry & Tomato Gazpacho, page 80, and follow it with Basil Ice Cream, page 208.

When I entertain outside, I make the dressing using a good-quality purchased mayonnaise, which is prepared with cooked eggs. And when I know the salad is going to be served under air conditioning, I prepare Homemade Mayonnaise, page 106, and add curry and chili powders. Both versions are equally delicious.

2 heads romaine lettuce, julienned

3 boneless, skinless organic whole chicken breasts, poached and cut into ¼-inch dice

6 stalks celery, cut into ¼-inch dice

2 large red tomatoes, peeled (see Box, page 133), and cut into ¼-inch dice

4 Golden Delicious apples, cut into ¼-inch dice

4 Hass avocados, pitted, peeled and cut into ¼-inch dice

3 ½ cups Curry Mayonnaise "Al Fresco," page 109, plus more for passing

FOR THE MATCHSTICK POTATOES:

4 medium Idaho potatoes

½ cup olive oil

Sea salt

In a medium bowl, toss the chicken with 1 cup of the Curry Mayonnaise. Set aside.

In a large glass bowl such as a punch bowl, layer the salad ingredients, spreading each with 2 tablespoons of the mayonnaise, beginning with the romaine lettuce, followed by the chicken, celery, tomatoes, apples and avocadoes. Spread the remaining mayonnaise on top, cover and refrigerate for 2 or 3 hours or overnight to allow the flavors to develop. Just before serving, fill a large bowl with cold, salted water. Peel the potatoes and, using a mandolin or food processor fitted with the julienne blade, cut the potatoes into matchsticks. Transfer the potatoes to the bowl of water to prevent them from discoloring.

In a large frying pan, heat the oil over high heat until smoking. Working in batches so as not to overcrowd the pan, fry the potatoes until crisp and golden, about 4 minutes. Using a slotted spoon, remove them from the pan and onto paper towels. Season with sea salt. Transfer to a baking sheet and into a warm oven while you fry the remaining potatoes.

Scatter the potatoes on top of the salad and serve.

SERVES 6 TO 8

Tomato Salad

In Palm Beach, we are fortunate to be near one of the original heirloom tomato farms in the country. Walter Ross started the resurrection of ancient tomato seeds years ago and has made a success out of his passion. Every Saturday morning from October through April, I go to the West Palm Beach farmers' market to purchase as many of Walter's Heirloom Tomatoes as I can carry. Walter is often at his stand dispensing tomato recipes and ideas, preaching about their cancer-fighting properties and giving samples of his tomatoes to anyone who wants a taste.

At home, I serve Walter's tomatoes sliced with a pinch of sea salt and a drizzle of olive oil. That's it. I do peel the tomatoes, especially when their skin tends to be thick. For elegant dinners, I might serve different colored tomatoes arranged in stacks and garnished with a single big basil leaf. For buffets, I cut them into thick slices and arrange them on a platter. For casual gatherings, I cut medium-size tomatoes into segments and serve them in a bowl. I tend to turn to mint when I am making this salad, since the combination reminds me of my childhood in Andalucia like no other.

No matter which way you present them, the key to any good tomato salad lies in the ripeness of the fruit. Choose those that are fragrant and semi-firm. Too soft and they fall apart when sliced, too firm and they have no flavor. I use a serrated bread knife to slice tomatoes very thinly and hold the end with a fork while doing so to get the last possible slice.

2 large red tomatoes, such Brandywine or Mortgage Lifter, peeled

2 large yellow tomatoes, such as Big Rainbow, peeled

2 large green tomatoes, such as Green Zebra, peeled

2 medium dark tomatoes, such as Black Krim or Cherokee Purple, peeled

Sea salt

1/4 cup extra-virgin olive oil

10 mint leaves

Slice the tomatoes into 1/4-inch rounds. Arrange the tomatoes on a rimmed platter and season with sea salt. Drizzle olive oil on top and garnish with the mint leaves.

SERVES 6 TO 8

HOW TO PEEL TOMATOES

Bring a large pot filled with about 4 inches of water to a boil over high heat. Meanwhile, using a sharp knife, score the bottom of each tomato in a cross shape. Working with one tomato at a time and using a slotted spoon, plunge it into the water for 30 seconds to loosen the skin. Transfer to a bowl. When cool enough to handle, remove the skin with your fingertips.

Duck Magret & Warm Onion Salad

Breasts of ducks are available in most supermarkets and most certainly at the local butcher. If you've never cooked duck, this is a great introduction to doing it without fear. The key is to sear the breasts, skin-side down, leaving them in the hot pan sufficiently long enough for the skin to become crispy. Do not be tempted to move them around in the pan or you will break the sear.

½ cup olive oil, divided

1 medium red onion, sliced into rings

1 medium white onion, sliced into rings

12 scallions, white and green parts only, cut into 3-inch pieces

½ cup balsamic vinegar

½ cup sherry vinegar

1 sprig thyme

6 boneless duck breasts, with skin

Sea salt and fresh ground pepper

1 pound mixed greens, such as baby spinach and mustard greens

---

In a large sauté pan, heat 4 tablespoons of olive oil over medium heat. Add the onions and sauté until translucent; about 3 minutes. Add the balsamic vinegar and 4 tablespoons of sherry vinegar and simmer until the onions become soft and dark. Remove from the heat and reserve.

Using a sharp knife, make a cross-hatch pattern on the skin of each duck breast. Season with salt and pepper. Heat the remaining olive oil in a pan over high heat and place the breasts skin-side down until the skin is crispy and golden; about 8 minutes. Turn onto its other side and cook for 2 minutes until medium rare. Transfer to a cutting board and rest for 2 minutes, reserving any juices. Slice the breasts on the diagonal in three pieces.

In a large bowl, toss the greens with the remaining olive oil and vinegar and arrange in a shallow serving platter. Top with the sautéed onions, duck breasts and pan juices. Serve warm.

SERVES 6

Ana Arias' Little Bits Salad

My friend Ana Arias, who grew up in Bilbao, Spain, gave me the recipe for this eclectic salad. We met while we were both working at Banco Bilbao Vizcaya in New York City. Ana was the brains behind the I.T. department and I was working on public relations projects. We have kept in touch throughout the years after discovering we have many friends—and a love of cooking— in common. At first, I was skeptical about the unusual combination of ingredients but I must admit to a change of heart the second I made it, which happened to be for a television appearance; I wanted to prepare something unexpected and colorful. Not only is it that, but it is delicious, as was made clear when the TV crew devoured every bit of it after taping was finished. For casual gatherings, I serve it in a ceramic majolica bowl. But when I want to make more of the presentation, I hollow out watermelons—tiny ones for sit-down meals and a nice, large single fruit for a buffet.

1 pound cherry tomatoes, washed, stemmed, and halved

1 pound white seedless grapes, washed and halved

1 6-ounce jar pitted black Kalamata olives, halved

½ pound feta cheese, crumbled

3 tablespoons olive oil

2 tablespoons balsamic vinegar

1 teaspoon Homemade Mayonnaise, page 106

Sea salt and fresh ground pepper

In a large salad bowl, combine the tomatoes, grapes, olives and feta cheese. In a small bowl, whisk together the olive oil, vinegar, mayonnaise, salt and pepper. Pour over the salad and toss to coat well. Cover and refrigerate until chilled. Serve cold.

SERVES 6

Prawn & Potato Salad with Warm Mustard Sauce

Tiger prawns, which are a bit bigger than jumbo shrimp, are always abundant in Florida, and make for an excellent warm first-course salad. In Andalucia, we reserve tiger prawns for salads such as this, while small shrimp are typically cooked al ajillo—with garlic— and bigger ones find themselves in paellas and seafood dishes. Use large prawns for this dish if you can find them; it will make a better presentation, more impressive and certainly more festive.

½ cup olive oil

Juice of 1 lemon

2 tablespoons Dijon mustard

6 medium red new potatoes

1 pound tiger prawns or jumbo shrimp (21/24), peeled and deveined

6 scallions, white and pale green parts only, thinly sliced

In a small bowl, whisk together 4 tablespoons of the olive oil, the lemon juice and the mustard. Set aside.

In a medium pot filled with salted water, boil the potatoes until fork tender, about 20 minutes. Drain in a colander and slice into ¼-inch rounds, but don't peel them. Arrange the potatoes on a shallow rimmed platter and drizzle with half the mustard sauce.

In a large sauté pan, heat the remaining olive oil over high heat. Add the shrimp and sauté until pink, about 2 minutes. Arrange over top of the potatoes, drizzling with remaining mustard sauce. Garnish with scallions and serve warm.

SERVES 6

Ensaladilla Rusa (Russian Salad)

This is the quintessential Spanish salad. Dressed with a vinegary mayonnaise, it is served in every tapas bar, restaurant and taberna throughout Spain. We grew up on Ensaladilla Rusa, especially in the summer; it was one of those dishes left in the fridge to nibble on when we came home from school or after a long afternoon of splashing in the pool. It is a perfect party dish and the ultimate in summer comfort food. It is so inbred in the culture of Spain that super-markets carry all the ingredients diced and chopped, very much like the prepared coleslaw in supermarkets here.

4 medium new potatoes

4 carrots, peeled and cut into ¼-inch dice

1 cup fresh or frozen peas, steamed

1 cup fresh or frozen haricots verts, steamed and cut into 1-inch pieces

½ cup pitted green olives, chopped

2 jarred roasted red peppers, drained and cut into ¼-inch dice

2 6-ounce cans albacore tuna, packed in oil, drained

2 cups Homemade Mayonnaise, page 106

3 medium hard-boiled eggs, sliced ¼-inch thick

Bring a large pot of salted water to a boil over high heat. Peel and cut the potatoes into ¼-inch dice. Place in a large bowl of water to prevent discoloration. Cook the potatoes until fork tender, about 20 minutes. Drain in a colander and set aside. Fill the same pot with salted water and bring to a boil; add the carrots and boil until tender. Drain and set aside.

In a large salad bowl, combine the potatoes, carrots, peas, beans, olives, pepper and tuna. Gently fold in the mayonnaise and mix until all of the ingredients are well coated. Smooth the top with a spatula. Arrange the slices of hard-boiled eggs on top. Cover and refrigerate until thoroughly chilled, about two hours.

SERVES 6

Main Courses

Eggplant, Béchamel & Tomato Gratin, PAGE 142

Three Vegetable Tortillas, PAGE 143

Huevos al Plato (Baked Eggs), PAGE 144

Huevos de la Casa, PAGE 145

Huevos a la Flamenca, PAGE 146

Gypsy Rice, PAGE 147

Prawns en Papillote, PAGE 148

Mussels with Curry Sauce, PAGE 150

Sea Bass with Salsa de Amontillado, PAGE 151

Porch House Striped Sea Bass, PAGE 152

Saucy Contessa Chicken, PAGE 153

Tagine of Chicken, Olives & Lemon, PAGE 155

Chicken in Champagne Sauce, PAGE 156

Breasts of Chicken with Sage & Serrano, PAGE 157

Cornish Game Hens with Lemon & Rosemary, PAGE 158

Lamb Chops with Fresh Herb Sauce, PAGE 159

Good Old-Fashioned Meatloaf, PAGE 160

Boneless Leg of Lamb a la Moruna, PAGE 162

Moussaka, PAGE 163

THE RECIPES IN THIS CHAPTER ARE SIMPLE IN TECHNIQUE BUT SOPHISTICATED IN FLAVOR AND PRESENTATION. JUST BECAUSE A

dish has few ingredients does not make it plebeian or rustic. The key is to choose those few ingredients with care, as all the flavor will come solely from them. Simple cooking techniques and great presentation can elevate even basic ingredients into elegant meals.

A good example is the egg. I often serve eggs for midweek suppers and as both a first course for dinner and an entrée for lunch during winter months. They remind me of dinners in the country where the main meal is at lunchtime and suppers are lighter fare. One of my favorite dinners is Huevos de la Casa, which literally translated means 'eggs from home.' It is the first dish I make when we come home from a long trip. Buy fresh organic eggs whenever possible; they will have a vibrant yolk and seem to cook faster than others. Organic eggs are not as large as their non-organic counterparts but their flavor is more intense.

Another foundation ingredient I adore is fish. It's so simple to prepare if you buy the freshest fish available. Finding an independent, knowledgeable fishmonger is the best route to fantastic fish; a top-notch dealer will sell you only the choicest catch. Fish requires little cooking — just a light brush with olive oil infused with herbs or lemon brings out its best flavor. Think about this when cooking for guests, though: Fish makes the whole house smell (sorry, but it is true). To assuage this fishy fragrance, light scented candles around the entranceway and living room before guests arrive.

When planning a party, I also turn to the kind of meat dishes that beg to be ignored. I have too much to do to fuss over any entrée — lighting candles, setting the table, preparing accompanying dishes and putting the children to bed all must be done before guests arrive — so I rarely make any labor-intensive meat dishes or ones that require heavy last-minute attention. My favorite recipes actually improve if left in the oven for longer than specified in the recipe, which happens frequently in my house.

Dinners with friends at home should be casual, intimate and cozy; a source of pleasure rather than panic. Begin your entertaining prowess with a few homemade dishes and then enhance them as you go along. Rely on the supermarket for desserts, cookies and breads. And do remember that friends are coming to your house to be with you, so just relax.

Perhaps the most exciting feature of the recipes here is that they are truly guidelines — consider them as inspiration and feel free to improvise as you see fit. Substituting ingredients is fine — I encourage it — so that you can put your own stamp on a recipe.

Eggplant, Béchamel & Tomato Gratin

This gratin is home-cooking at its best. While the ingredient list may seem long, the gratin is a cinch to prepare once the ingredients are ready. Put the gratin together ahead of time up to the point where you add the eggs; do this step just before baking.

2 cups Tomato Sauce, puréed, page 116

Olive oil for frying

4 large eggplants

1 dozen eggs

2 tablespoons butter

3 tablespoons flour, plus more for dredging

1 ½ cups milk

Pinch of salt and fresh ground pepper

Pinch of nutmeg

1 cup each grated mozzarella and Parmesan cheese

Preheat the oven to 350°F. Slice the eggplants into ½-inch rounds and place in a bowl of salted water. In a small bowl, whisk 4 of the eggs. Place the dredging flour on a dinner plate. Fill a large frying pan with a ½-inch of olive oil and set over high heat. Working in batches, dry the eggplant slices and dredge them first in the egg and then in the flour; shake off the excess. Fry the eggplant slices in oil, turning once, until golden. Continue with remaining eggplant slices.

In a saucepan, heat the butter over medium-high heat and add the 3 tablespoons flour, stirring constantly until it is dissolved. Slowly add the milk and continue stirring until the sauce bubbles and thickens to make a béchamel. Season with salt, pepper and nutmeg. Set aside.

In an 8x11 ovenproof dish, assemble the gratin. Pour half of the tomato sauce on the bottom of the dish. Arrange half of the eggplant slices over it, followed by the mozzarella and half of the béchamel sauce. Top with the remaining eggplant slices and the tomato sauce, followed by the béchamel sauce and the Parmesan. Make 8 evenly spaced indentations and crack an egg in each, sprinkle with salt and bake until bubbly; aproximately 15 minutes. Serve hot.

SERVES 8

Three Vegetable Tortillas

This dish is a staple for entertaining at home. This is the vegetable version, but it can also be made with tuna fish, spaghetti or potatoes. It is an ideal buffet offering and also makes a lovely first course. At home, I serve these tortillas one on top of another, covered in Pink Béchamel Sauce, page 110.

¼ cup olive oil

10 ounces fresh spinach, stems removed

3 medium zucchini, cut into ½-inch dice

2 medium eggplants, cut into ½-inch dice

1 dozen large eggs

2 cups Pink Béchamel Sauce, page 110

Pinch of salt and fresh ground pepper

In a large skillet over high heat, heat one tablespoon olive oil. Add the spinach and sauté until wilted and all the moisture evaporates, about 3 minutes. Season with salt. Transfer the spinach to a cutting board and chop roughly.

In the same skillet, add another tablespoon of oil and heat until hot. Add the zucchini and sauté until soft. Season with salt and transfer to a plate. Add the last tablespoon of olive oil and heat until hot. Add the eggplant and sauté until soft. Season with salt and set aside.

In a medium bowl, whisk 4 eggs. Add the spinach and mix to incorporate. In a non-stick 8-inch sauté pan, heat one tablespoon olive oil. Pour the egg and spinach mixture into the hot pan. Cook until the edges turn golden brown and the tortilla can be shaken easily from the pan. Slide the tortilla onto a plate and flip it onto the other side back into the pan. Cook until the eggs are set. Keep warm in the oven while you make the others. Repeat using the zucchini and the eggplant.

Place the three tortillas on top of each other in a round serving platter and pour the hot pink béchamel sauce over the tortillas, letting it trickle down the sides. Serve hot.

SERVES 6

Huevos al Plato (Baked Eggs)

This dish is traditionally made in individual gratin dishes. They are hard to find, as baked eggs are out of fashion right now, but I have been lucky to discover sets at estate sales. Some of the dishes are very ornate and have beautiful imagery on the outside; others have solid-color enamel outside and white ceramic inside. It's not uncommon to find plain white ones, too. Since this recipe can be assembled ahead of time, it is great as a first course for a group, or as a main course for a midweek supper.

4 tablespoons olive oil

1 large onion, diced

4 cloves of garlic, diced

2 medium eggplants, diced

4 medium zucchini, diced

1 16-ounce can diced tomatoes

1 16-ounce can tomato purée

3 tablespoons fresh rosemary leaves, minced

1 bay leaf

Sea salt and fresh ground pepper

6 large eggs

In a medium stockpot, heat the olive oil over high heat and add the onions and garlic; season with a little salt. Sauté until the onions are translucent. Reduce the heat to medium-low and add the eggplant. Cook until it begins to soften and turn golden on the edges. Add the zucchini and continue cooking until the zucchini begins to release its liquid and becomes soft. Add the diced tomatoes with their liquid, the tomato purée, rosemary and bay leaf. Simmer, stirring occasionally, until the sauce thickens and all the vegetables are cooked through.

Preheat the oven to 400°F. In a shallow gratin dish or in 6 individual ones, spread the eggplant and tomato sauce in the bottom of the dish. Crack an egg in the middle of individual gratins or evenly spaced around a larger gratin dish. Bake until the sauce is bubbly and the eggs are cooked to your liking. I cook mine for about 15 minutes.

SERVES 6

Huevos de la Casa

This is a very easy dish to double or reduce as needed. As the main course for dinner, I cook two eggs per person. For a first course, I serve one per person.

6 slices country white or whole wheat bread

Olive oil for frying

2 tablespoons butter

1 small onion, finely diced

2 cloves of garlic, finely chopped

4 slices Serrano or baked ham, finely chopped

2 tablespoons flour

2 cups milk

1 teaspoon grated nutmeg

Salt and fresh ground pepper

4 tablespoons heavy cream

6 large eggs

In a frying pan or deep fryer, place about ½ inch of olive oil and heat until hot. Working in batches, fry the bread until golden, turning once. Drain on paper towels and place on a round serving platter.

In a saucepan, heat the butter over medium-high heat until hot. Add the onions and garlic and sauté until soft. Add the ham and cook for two minutes. Sprinkle with flour and stir well to combine. Pour in the milk and bring to a boil, stirring constantly, until the mixture thickens. Season with nutmeg, salt and pepper to taste. Add the cream and stir well to combine. Cover to keep warm until the eggs are ready.

In an egg poacher, bring water to a boil. Spray each cavity with cooking spray or lightly coat with olive oil. Place one egg in each cavity and cover with a lid. Cook for exactly 4 minutes. Remove the eggs from the heat and place on top of the fried bread. Cover with the cream sauce and serve hot.

SERVES 6

Huevos a la Flamenca

Make this dish with early spring vegetables. If you like, add baby artichokes, green beans, pearl onions or even lima beans. It is a colorful and delicious dish, perfect for a midweek supper. I like serving it in a cazuela, *in keeping with its rustic characteristics, but any oven-to-table dish works.*

1 pound thick bacon, diced

1 pound chorizo, finely sliced

4 tablespoons olive oil

1 small onion, diced

1 clove of garlic, sliced

1 16-ounce can diced tomatoes

10 asparagus tips, each about 3 inches long

1 pound fresh or frozen small peas

½ cup Beef Stock, page 101

6 large eggs

Salt and fresh ground pepper

In a frying pan over medium heat, fry the bacon and the chorizo until all the fat is released and both are crispy. Drain on paper towels and set aside.

Preheat the oven to 400°F. In an earthenware *cazuela* or any stove-to-oven dish, heat the olive oil over medium-low heat. Add the onions and garlic and sauté until transparent and soft. Drain about half the liquid from the diced tomatoes and add to the onion mixture. Add the asparagus and simmer until some of the liquid evaporates. Add the peas and stir to combine. Add the stock and simmer for 5 minutes. Using tongs, arrange the asparagus spears decoratively in the dish. Using a large spoon, make 8 evenly spaced indentations in the tomato mixture. Crack an egg into each indentation and season with salt and pepper. Scatter the bacon and chorizo over the dish and bake until the eggs are cooked to your liking. I prefer that they are set, which is about 12 to 15 minutes. If you are making this in a *cazuela,* you may cook the eggs on the stove top; just cover the *cazuela* to speed the process. Serve hot and bubbly.

SERVES 4 AS A MAIN COURSE, 6 AS A FIRST COURSE

Gypsy Rice

When I make Gypsy Rice, I have romantic visions of a gypsy caravan stopping for the night, cooking over an open fire, dancing and singing flamenco all night. It's not something I can replicate in my garden, so I console myself by listening to flamenco music and dancing in the kitchen as I cook!

You can add chopped ham, chicken or fish, but I like this version best. I make this in large paella pans or in earthenware cazuelas *that I bring right to the table.*

2 tablespoons olive oil

2 tablespoons butter

1 large white onion, chopped

2 tomatoes, diced

4 cloves of garlic, chopped

1 cup sherry or white wine

2 cups of Chicken Stock page 100, or Shellfish Stock, page 102

1 cup rice

2 pounds shrimp, shelled and deveined

1 pound bay scallops, halved

½ cup parsley, chopped

Salt and fresh ground pepper

In a large shallow sauté or paella pan, heat the olive oil and butter over medium-high heat. Add the onions and garlic and sauté until soft. Add the tomatoes and cook for one minute until soft. Add the rice and stir to coat well. Add the chicken stock and sherry and bring to a boil. Add the shrimp and scallops and season with salt and pepper. Bring to a boil. Reduce the heat to medium and cook, uncovered, for about 10 minutes. Cover and continue to cook for an additional 10 minutes or until the rice is tender. Remove from the heat and stir in the fresh parsley. Serve warm.

SERVES 6

Prawns en Papillote

Making these lovely packages is not as complicated as it looks. And, even though there is cream in the recipe, serving seafood en papillote is a wonderfully healthy approach (one cup divided among eight people makes only two tablespoons of cream per serving — no big deal in my opinion!). Serve a vegetable soup to start, such as Tomato & Plum Gazpacho, page 79. Warm Pineapple with Maple Syrup, page 205, brings the menu to an elegant conclusion.

24 prawns or jumbo shrimp (3 per person), peeled and deveined

2 medium zucchini, julienned

3 medium yellow squash, julienned

4 large carrots, peeled and julienned

Juice of two lemons

8 tablespoons olive oil

½ cup white wine or sherry

Salt and fresh ground pepper

8 pieces organic parchment paper

FOR THE CREAM SAUCE (MAKES 1 ½ CUPS):

1 teaspoon butter

1 teaspoon olive oil

1 small onion, finely chopped

1 cup heavy cream

1 tomato, peeled and finely chopped

Salt and fresh ground pepper

In a small pan, heat the butter and oil over medium-high heat. Add the onions and sauté until soft and translucent. Add the heavy cream and bring to a boil, stirring so that it doesn't overflow the pot, about 3 minutes. Add the tomatoes and season with salt and pepper. Serve hot.

Preheat the oven to 350°F. In a bowl, combine the zucchini, squash and carrots. Place three prawns in the center of a piece of parchment paper and top with one-eighth of the vegetables. Sprinkle

with lemon juice, white wine (or sherry) and one tablespoon of olive oil. Season with salt and pepper. Repeat with remaining vegetables and shrimp. Close the packages, making a double fold on top and folding the ends underneath or tie the ends with kitchen string to close the packages. Place on a cookie sheet and bake for 15 minutes. Serve in the packages, letting your guests open the parcels at the table with the cream sauce in a gravy boat or small serving vessel.

SERVES 8

Mussels with Curry Sauce

When I can find small Prince Edward Island mussels (I don't like the really big fleshy ones), I make this dish as a main course. It is flavorful and a great crowd pleaser. I serve it in a big bowl with a spoon to scoop up the juices and place it in the center of the table for all to dig in. A large baguette to mop up juices is essential. Dry white wine is the perfect accompaniment. Serve a cheese course, followed by fresh fruit for a perfect meal.

4 tablespoons olive oil

1 large onion, diced

2 cloves of garlic, diced

4 celery stalks, diced

3 tablespoons curry powder

Sea salt and fresh ground pepper

1 cup heavy cream

4 pounds mussels, cleaned and rinsed in two changes of water

10 scallions, diced

In a large sauté pan, heat the olive oil over high heat. Add the onions, garlic and celery and sauté until soft and slightly browned, about 8 minutes. Add the curry and sauté to release the aroma. Season with salt and pepper. Add the cream and bring to a boil. Reduce the heat to low, add the mussels and cover until they open, 8 to 10 minutes.

To serve, transfer the mussels with their liquid to a large bowl. Sprinkle with scallions just before serving.

SERVES 8

Sea Bass with Salsa de Amontillado

Amontillado is a type of sherry from Spain. Golden, sweet, rich and nutty, it pairs beautifully with a touch of olive oil, carrots and cream to create a rustic sauce that is full of flavor. Reserve a little sauce to serve alongside the fish or to pour on top after it comes out of the oven.

Fresh fish really needs little help to bring out its flavor; the salsa is just a touch of "something" to dress it up a bit. The fish may be prepared an hour or so before friends arrive and finished just as they sit down to the table. Have the sauce ready to go and you can assemble the whole dish in seconds.

8 tablespoons olive oil

2 carrots, peeled and julienned or grated in the food processor

1 large onion, finely diced

1 cup heavy cream

1 cup amontillado sherry

Salt and fresh ground pepper

10 pounds sea bass, cut into 10 steaks (1 pound per serving, 2 extra)

½ cup flour

¼ cup parsley, finely chopped

Preheat the oven to 350°F. In a large sauté pan, heat the olive oil over high heat. Add the carrots and onions and sauté until the onions become translucent. Add the heavy cream and amontillado and bring to a boil. Reduce the heat to medium and simmer for 2 minutes. Taste and season with salt and fresh ground pepper. Set aside.

Dredge the sea bass steaks with a little flour, shaking off the excess. In a large sauté pan, heat 4 tablespoons olive oil over high heat. Working in batches, add the steaks and sauté for 4 minutes, turning once, just until the fish turns golden. Transfer the steaks to an ovenproof serving dish. Pour the amontillado sauce over and bake for 12 minutes. Garnish with parsley and serve.

SERVES 8

Porch House Striped Sea Bass

My husband Minot loves to go fishing in Southampton. He casts from the beach and often brings home striped bass. He is only allowed to keep fish bigger than 26 inches so we regularly invite friends to share our bounty. I got the idea for this dish from a tiny, out-of-the-way restaurant in Palmones, a small seaside town near Gibraltar, but I have named this recipe Porch House, in honor of our house in Southampton.

½ cup mild olive oil

3 cloves of garlic, sliced

1 teaspoon salt and pepper

Juice of 2 lemons

3 sprigs dill, about ½ cup

1 lemon, sliced thin for garnish

1 26-inch striped bass, cleaned and deboned

Preheat the oven to 350°F. In a small bowl, mix the olive oil, garlic, salt, pepper and lemon juice. Set aside.

Place the fish on a large baking tray or a cookie sheet. Open the fish carefully so as not to break the uncut side. Drizzle with the olive oil mixture, spread the dill around and top with the lemon slices. Close the fish and season the outside with a large pinch of sea salt. Bake until the fish is opaque, about 20 minutes.

To serve, transfer the fish to a decorative platter and slice into 2-inch pieces. Garnish with additional lemon.

SERVES 8

Saucy Contessa Chicken

I love this flavorful dish any time of year. It is delicious, easy to make and the right size for a crowd. This recipe is based on Chicken Tagine, page 155, but has a different cooking method: it is baked in the oven. Serve it with grilled vegetables, Gnocchi a la Romana, page 171, or Mashed Potatoes en Croûte, page 174, for a sensational dinner.

4 tablespoons olive oil

6 organic chicken legs, skin on

6 organic chicken thighs, skin on

Salt and fresh ground pepper

1 small yellow onion, diced

4 tablespoons fresh ginger, peeled and chopped

4 cloves of garlic, diced

½ cup dry white wine

3 cups Chicken Stock, page 100

Pinch saffron

1 lemon, sliced

1 bay leaf

½ cup parsley, chopped

Preheat the oven to 350°F. Season the chicken pieces with salt and pepper. In a large sauté pan, heat the olive oil over high heat until hot. Add the chicken, skin-side down, and sauté until golden, about 5 minutes per side. Transfer the chicken to an ovenproof dish.

In the same sauté pan over high heat, add the onion, ginger and garlic. Sauté until fragrant and translucent. Add the wine and cook until reduced by half. In a saucepan, bring the broth to a simmer. Using your fingers, shred the saffron and dissolve in the broth. Pour the broth over the chicken pieces, top with the garlic and ginger mixture and surround the dish with the lemon slices. Add the bay leaf and bake until the chicken's juices run clear when pierced with a fork, about 1 hour. To serve, remove the bay leaf and garnish with chopped parsley.

SERVES 10

Tagine of Chicken, Olives & Lemon

The tagine, a conical shaped pot typical of Moroccan cooking, is essential to make this dish. Its shape is what gives gives the food the unique flavor. It also makes for a great presentation at the table or buffet.

4 tablespoons olive oil

4 organic chicken legs, skin on

4 organic chicken thighs, skin on

Salt and fresh ground pepper

1 2-inch piece fresh ginger, peeled and finely chopped

1 small onion, diced

1 clove of garlic, minced

2 cups Chicken Stock, page 100

Pinch saffron

1 lemon, finely sliced

1 cup green olives, drained

1 cup parsley, roughly chopped

Season the chicken pieces with salt and pepper. Place the tagine over medium heat. Add the butter and oil and heat until the butter is melted. Add the chicken pieces and brown until the skin is light golden. Add the ginger, onion and garlic. In a small saucepan, heat the stock. Using your fingers, shred the saffron into the warm stock and pour over the chicken. Arrange the lemon slices between the chicken pieces. Reduce the heat, cover and simmer for 1 hour. Add the olives and taste for seasoning. Continue cooking for another 30 minutes. Remove the lid and simmer an additional 15 minutes, or until most of the juices have evaporated. Garnish with parsley and serve.

SERVES 4

Chicken in Champagne Sauce

This is my sister Cristina's recipe. She makes it every year for Christmas. I also make it on special occasions, particularly when I have a few open bottles of Champagne left over from a dinner party. It also works with other birds like pheasant, Cornish game hen and partridge. Serve it with fluffy white rice or simple risotto to mop up the delicious juices.

It is a great entertaining dish, as the birds must be marinated overnight or at least 12 hours for the Champagne to do its magic and imbue the meat with its flavor and aroma. Cava or prosecco can be substituted for the Champagne.

2 whole organic chickens with skin, cut into 6 pieces each (breasts cut in half)

1 bottle of Champagne

2 white onions, roughly chopped

1 bay leaf

10 to 15 whole peppercorns

1 cup all-purpose flour

½ cup olive oil

Salt and fresh ground pepper

In a shallow ovenproof dish, combine the chicken with the Champagne, onions, bay leaf and peppercorns. Marinate overnight or for at least 12 hours.

Preheat the oven to 350°F. Take the chicken pieces out of the marinade and dry on paper towels. Reserve the marinade. Dredge the chicken pieces in flour, shaking off the excess. In a large frying pan, heat 4 tablespoons of olive oil over high heat and add the chicken pieces. Working in batches, sauté until golden brown all over. Add more olive oil as needed. Place the chicken in the reserved oven dish with the marinade. Bake for 30 to 45 minutes until the chicken is no longer pink.

Remove the chicken from the oven dish and place on a warm serving platter. Remove the bay leaf from the marinade and discard. In a blender, purée the marinade and strain through a medium sieve. Reheat before serving and pour over the chicken pieces.

SERVES 8

Breasts of Chicken with Sage & Serrano

Wrapping breasts of chicken with sage and Serrano ham imbues an otherwise unremarkable meat with delicious flavor. This dish demands a grand presentation. It goes well with all sorts of accompaniments, from Mashed Potato en Croûte, page 174, to Smashed Peas with Mint, page 184. A light dessert like Torta de Santiago, page 200, is the perfect ending.

8 skinless breasts of chicken, preferably organic

Salt and fresh ground pepper

32 sage leaves

8 slices Serrano ham

4 tablespoons olive oil

Preheat the oven to 350°F. Season each breast with salt and pepper and top each with 4 sage leaves. Wrap one piece of ham around each breast leaving the "seam" on the bottom.

Arrange the chicken in an oven dish coated with olive oil. Bake for 20 minutes or until the juices run clear.

To serve, cut into 2-inch pieces and place on a platter.

SERVES 6 TO 8

Cornish Game Hens with Lemon & Rosemary

This easy-to-cook method works well with chicken too. Use small organic Cornish game hens and serve them with Salsa Española, page 111, on the side. Round out the menu with a green salad, Garden Vegetables with Tarragon Butter, page 183, and Smashed Potatoes with Rosemary, page 173, for a delicious dinner.

6 Cornish game hens

4 lemons

6 3-inch sprigs of fresh rosemary

6 tablespoons olive oil

Salt and fresh ground pepper

Preheat the oven to 450°F. Rub the Cornish game hens with one tablespoon olive oil mixed with the juice of one of the lemons. Season with salt and pepper and stuff half a lemon and the rosemary sprig into each cavity. Place in a large roasting pan and roast for about 45 minutes, or until the juices run clear. Allow the hens to rest for 10 minutes. Slice each hen in half using kitchen scissors. Trim away the dark backbones. Remove the lemons and the rosemary sprigs.

To serve, arrange the hens skin-side up on a platter. Drizzle with pan juices.

SERVES 6

Lamb Chops with Fresh Herb Sauce

Baby racks of lamb are a treat, especially when I can find organic ones. They are so naturally tender and delicious they need few enhancements. This herb sauce gives the lamb chops extra moisture and brightens the plate a bit. Try this sauce as a marinade for skirt steaks or veal chops — it pairs well with them. Poolside in the summer, I serve these lamb chops next to Spaghetti with Fresh Tomato & Basil, page 172. For a cozy winter dinner, I serve them with Potato Gratin with Salsa Española, page 176, and Golden Onions, page 179.

3 racks baby lamb chops (about 6 pieces each)

Salt and fresh ground pepper

1 cup Fresh Herb Sauce, page 113

Preheat the oven to 350°F. Season the racks with salt and pepper. Spread the Fresh Herb Sauce over the fatty side of the lamb. Set aside for 15 to 20 minutes. Place the racks on an oven tray or on a cookie sheet lined with parchment paper. Bake for 20 – 25 minutes for rare; bake a few minutes longer for medium-rare. Let the lamb rest for 10 minutes. Slice the rack into individual cutlets and arrange on a serving platter.

SERVES 6 TO 8

Good Old-Fashioned Meatloaf

When I make this meatloaf, I sometimes make it freeform and other times cook it in loaf pans for a neater presentation. I do make it in large quantities as it freezes beautifully. For extra flavor, substitute ground sausage for 1 pound of any of the meats.

3 tablespoons olive oil

1 large onion, diced

3 celery stalks, diced

2 cloves of garlic, diced

6 slices bread, cubed

2 ½ cups Tomato Sauce, page 116

1 cup milk

1 cup parsley, finely chopped

1 cup grated Parmesan cheese

1 tablespoon Worcestershire sauce

1 pound ground beef chuck or round

1 pound ground veal

1 pound ground pork

1 pound ground turkey

Salt and fresh ground pepper

½ pound bacon

Preheat the oven to 350°F. In a sauté pan, heat the olive oil over high heat. Add the onions, celery and garlic and sauté until soft. In a large bowl, combine the bread, 1 ½ cups of the tomato sauce and the milk. Stir well to combine. Add the parsley, cheese, Worcestershire sauce, meats, onion mixture and salt and pepper. Mix gently with your fingers to combine well. Shape the mixture to resemble a large loaf or two smaller ones and place on a baking tray. Arrange the bacon slices on a diagonal to cover the loaf or loaves. Tuck the ends of the bacon under the meat. Pour one cup of the tomato sauce on top. Bake for one hour. Drain some of the fat from the pan and bake 30 minutes more. Let rest for 5 minutes before slicing. Slice into 1 ½-inch thick slices and serve hot.

SERVES 8 TO 10

Boneless Leg of Lamb a la Moruna

This recipe is a prime example of the Moorish legacy in Spain. Mixing sweet spices and nuts with meat is typical Moroccan cooking. It makes a flavorful, unexpected alternative to traditional roast lamb. It must marinate 6 to 8 hours or overnight — plan accordingly.

1 cup golden raisins or a combination of dried fruits, chopped the same size as raisins

1 cup dry fino sherry

4 pounds loin of lamb, de-boned and cut into 8 pieces

20 pitted dates

4 tablespoons peeled almonds

1 teaspoon ground cinnamon

½ teaspoon ground cumin

2 tablespoons olive oil

2 large onions, diced

3 cloves of garlic, chopped

2 cups Chicken Stock, page 100

Salt and fresh ground pepper

In a bowl, combine the raisins or other dried fruits with the sherry and soak for about 30 minutes, or until the fruits are plump. In a large bowl or a large resealable plastic bag, combine the lamb pieces, almonds, raisins-and-sherry mixture, cinnamon, cumin, olive oil, onions and garlic. Season with salt and pepper. Toss to coat the lamb pieces well and place in the refrigerator to marinate at least 6 hours.

Remove the meat from the bag or bowl, reserving the marinade. Heat 2 tablespoons olive oil in a large sauté pan until hot. Add the lamb and brown, turning once. Add the dried fruits and marinade to the pan and simmer until the liquid evaporates. Just as all of the liquid evaporates, add the stock and bring to a boil. Reduce the heat and simmer until the lamb is cooked through and tender, 45 – 60 minutes. To serve, remove the meat from the pan, slice into 1-inch pieces and spoon the fruit sauce on top. Garnish with additional raisins.

SERVES 8 TO 10

Moussaka

Serve Moussaka in early spring, when the auguries of summer begin to appear. It is sensational with Smashed Peas with Mint, page 184, and later in the season with Tomato Salad, page 132.

3 tablespoons olive oil

1 white onion, diced

4 cloves of garlic, chopped

3 pounds ground lamb

Sea salt

2 teaspoons ground cinnamon

1 teaspoon grated nutmeg

2 sprigs rosemary

2 cups tomato sauce

2 bay leaves

3 eggplants

1 cup each grated mozzarella and Parmesan cheese

In a sauté pan, heat the olive oil over medium heat. Add the onion and garlic and sauté until soft and translucent. Add the ground lamb and a generous pinch of sea salt. Cook until the lamb is no longer pink, stirring and breaking the meat with a fork. Add the cinnamon, nutmeg, rosemary sprigs, tomato sauce and bay leaves. Bring to a boil. Reduce the heat to low and simmer until the liquid has reduced and thickens, about 35 minutes. (Remove the rosemary sprigs and bay leaf before assembling).

While the sauce is cooking, preheat the oven to 350°F. Slice the eggplants into ½-inch rounds. Place in a single layer on a cookie sheet, sprinkle with salt and drizzle with olive oil. Bake in the oven in batches, if necessary, until just soft, 10 – 15 minutes.

In an ovenproof dish, layer the ingredients beginning with the eggplant, mozzarella cheese and meat sauce; top with more eggplant and finish with Parmesan. Bake until the cheese is melted and the top is golden, about 30 minutes.

SERVES 8

Side Dishes

Shrimp Fideoada, PAGE 168

Fusilli with Shrimp, Garlic & Lemon, PAGE 169

Gnocchi a la Romana, PAGE 171

Spaghetti with Fresh Tomato & Basil, PAGE 172

Smashed Potatoes with Rosemary, PAGE 173

Mashed Potatoes en Croûte, PAGE 174

Potato Gratin with Salsa Española, PAGE 176

Baby Bok Choy, PAGE 177

Ginger Carrots, PAGE 178

Golden Onions, PAGE 179

Eggplant Bundles with Goat Cheese, PAGE 181

Sautéed Spinach with Raisins & Pine Nuts, PAGE 182

Garden Vegetables with Tarragon Butter, PAGE 183

Smashed Peas with Mint, PAGE 184

Salt-Roasted Winter Vegetables, PAGE 185

SIDE DISHES ARE THE ACCESSORIES THAT COMPLEMENT, ADORN AND ENHANCE THE MAIN EVENT, VERY

much like a gracious shawl over a simple evening dress or a fantastic belt over a plain tunic. These dishes add color, sparkle and goodness to each meal. Some are so good by themselves, they can double as a first course and others beg to be an accompaniment. They are here together because they are my favorite ones. Not really serious discrimination, just personal taste.

I've served every dish in this chapter dozens of times and always with great success. Pasta, potatoes and vegetables comprise the recipes here, each one uncomplicated yet capitalizing on the ingredients' fresh flavor. The beauty of the pasta dishes is that they can move around the plate, from the side to the center, either as a first course or, in some instances, as a main course. It all depends on your mood, your guests and just how hungry you all are. For example, the Shrimp Fideoada is typically served as a first course, but it can very easily become a hearty side dish to simple grilled meats. The same goes for the other two pasta offerings: Fusilli with Shrimp, Garlic & Lemon and Spaghetti with Tomato & Basil are soul-satisfying main courses or they can make a nice duo on a buffet. The potato recipes — smashed and crisped, mashed and encased in a golden crust, and gratinéed — are always hands-down favorites.

After all, what's not to love about comforting potatoes, a bit of butter and a touch of cream?

In the vegetable dishes, you have an opportunity to add glorious color to the dinner table or buffet, not to mention a healthy dose of vitamins and minerals. In fact, when we eat at home, I often make several vegetable dishes for dinner, such as Baby Bok Choy, page 177, and Salt-Roasted Winter Vegetables. They're remarkably filling yet don't leave you feeling weighed down. For a crowd, a selection of vegetable side dishes enlivens a buffet — and gives guests options for composing their own meal. On some occasions, I like to approach my menu with an eye toward color, especially when it comes to vegetables. For example, I will serve a platter of all different kinds of green vegetables including broccoli florets, asparagus, green beans, zucchini and spinach. Or, I will use all yellow ones including grilled onions, yellow zucchini, peppers and tomatoes. On the other hand, when I serve a simple steak, I adorn the dish with every colored vegetable I can find. Whatever the case, always choose vegetables that are in season and, whenever possible, locally grown.

Eating whatever is in season has terrific health advantages. Most fruits and vegetables have a six-week peak growing season and, having been ripened on the tree or vine, they contain more nutrients than those shipped green from afar. Try something new once in a while. You will be amazed.

Shrimp Fideoada

Fideo is the Spanish word for noodle. In this Catalan dish, the pasta is cooked in the pan juices, full of onion and beef stock, drinking up their savory flavors, somewhat in the way risotto absorbs the liquid in which it is cooked. The method creates a juicy, robust dish. It makes a lovely side dish or first course followed by a hearty main course meat dish.

3 tablespoons olive oil

1 medium onion, diced

2 cloves of garlic, chopped

2 pounds mixed wild mushrooms, thinly sliced

1 tablespoon crushed red pepper

Sea salt and fresh ground pepper

1 pound dry spaghetti, broken in half

4 cups Beef Stock, page 101

1 pound large (31-35) shrimp, peeled and deveined

½ cup parsley, roughly chopped, for garnish

In a large sauté pan, heat the olive oil over medium-high heat. Add the onions and garlic until soft, about 3 minutes. Add the mushrooms and red pepper and sauté until the mushrooms begin to release all their juices and they become slightly soft, about 8 minutes. Season with salt and pepper. Add the spaghetti and stir to coat well with the pan juices. Pour in the broth, making sure it covers the spaghetti. Bring to a boil. Reduce the heat to medium-low and simmer for 8 minutes. Add the shrimp and cook, covered, until the shrimp are pink and the pasta is cooked al dente, 5 to 6 minutes. Transfer the pasta and its juices to a large, shallow, rimmed platter. Sprinkle with parsley and serve.

SERVES 8

Fusilli with Shrimp, Garlic & Lemon

I adore pasta dishes in which the sauce cooks while the pasta boils. To me, these dishes are perfect for entertaining crowds as they are quick to cook and easy to make. This is one of three different pasta dishes I prepare for a buffet-style gathering for a big crowd. Accompanied by two simple salads—a mixed green one and a toss of sliced tomatoes—several different artisanal breads and a cheese platter featuring a blue cheese, a hard cheese and a soft cheese, the pastas make fine main courses. It's really quite uncomplicated yet bountiful. In this dish, add more or less of the flavors you like—it is wonderfully flexible that way. I prefer intense flavors, so don't be shy with the garlic, and spicy red peppers.

1 pound fusilli pasta

1 cup olive oil

4 cloves of garlic, chopped

1 pound large (31-35) shrimp, peeled and deveined

1 teaspoon crushed red pepper

Juice and zest of 1 lemon

20 basil leaves, thinly sliced

In a large pot filled with boiling water, cook the pasta al dente, 12-14 minutes. Drain, return to the pot and toss with two tablespoons of the olive oil. Cover to keep warm.

While the pasta is cooking heat 6 tablespoons of the olive oil in a large sauté pan over medium-high heat. Add the garlic and sauté until slightly golden, about 1 minute. Add the shrimp, red pepper flakes, lemon juice and zest. Season with salt and pepper. Cook, stirring often, until the shrimp turns pink. Stir in the basil and the reserved pasta. Heat through, adding more olive oil if needed to coat the pasta. Serve warm.

SERVES 8

Gnocchi a la Romana

This is one of my beloved childhood comfort foods. It has a wonderful rib-sticking quality. Work the semolina until it separates from the pan so it is cooked through, then spread it quickly on a cookie sheet. I cut the dough using a 3-inch round cutter but it is also fun to use holiday-themed cutters when the occasion calls for it. If you prefer polenta, by all means substitute it for the semolina. The best part of making this dish? The leftovers (if there are any!) are divine the next day, reheated and served with a mixed green salad.

4 cups whole milk

4 cups water

3 cups quick-cooking semolina flour

Pinch of salt

Pinch of nutmeg

Fresh ground pepper

2 cups Parmesan cheese, grated

3 egg yolks

3 tablespoons butter plus more for the baking dish

In a medium stockpot, combine the milk and water and bring to a gentle boil over high heat. Add the semolina, salt, nutmeg and black pepper and cook for 3-4 minutes until the semolina has absorbed the milk and becomes thick enough for a wooden spoon to stand up in. Reduce the heat to medium-low and, using a wooden spoon, stir vigorously until the semolina releases easily from the sides of the pot. Add 1 cup of the Parmesan and the egg yolks and stir until well combined. Remove from the heat and, using a spatula, spread on a cold surface such as marble or a cookie sheet to an even thickness, about ½ inch. Let cool completely.

Preheat the oven to 400°F. Butter a 4-quart oven-to-table dish. Cut the dough into medallions using a cookie cutter or a glass and place them in the buttered dish, overlapping them slightly like scalloped potatoes. Sprinkle with the remaining grated cheese and dot with butter. Bake for 20 minutes or until the tops become crispy and golden. Let rest a few minutes; serve very hot.

SERVES 6

Spaghetti with Fresh Tomato & Basil

*This is one of the first pasta recipes I learned to make when I moved to New York, and it
has never left my repertoire. Everyone loves it. Period. As in the Fusilli with Shrimp, Garlic &
Lemon, page 169, I love that I can make the sauce at the same time as the water boils.
Alternatively, you can make this sauce ahead of time, which allows for the garlic and basil
to infuse their flavor into the oil, but it is just as delicious made at the last minute. Serve it family-
style in an oversize bowl and accompany with a hearty loaf of bread and a green salad.*

4 red heirloom tomatoes, peeled (see Box, page 133) and diced

2 cloves of garlic, chopped

5 scallions, white and light green parts only, chopped

1 pound fresh mozzarella, diced

1 cup extra virgin olive oil

1 teaspoon crushed red pepper

½ cup basil, finely chopped

Sea salt and fresh ground pepper

1 pound spaghetti

In a large bowl, combine the tomatoes, garlic, scallions, mozzarella and olive oil. Season with
salt and pepper and set aside.

Bring a large pot of salted water to a boil. Add the spaghetti and cook until al dente, about
8 minutes. Drain in a colander and return to the pot. Add the tomato mixture and toss to combine.
Add the crushed red pepper and basil, stir to incorporate, and serve.

SERVES 6 TO 8

Smashed Potatoes with Rosemary

This is an ideal dish in which to include children, as it is a bit like making mud pies! Little ones love to do the smashing part of the job, which is essential for exposing as much potato as possible to the high heat, resulting in a super crisp shell encasing creamy potatoes. When the potatoes are soft, I use a meat mallet, the back of a spoon and even my fist to "smash" or press the potatoes into patties. A drizzle of olive oil, a sprinkle of sea salt and a pinch of rosemary is all it takes to elevate them to dinner party status.

- 2 pounds white, red or purple baby potatoes
- 2 sprigs fresh rosemary, needles stripped and chopped
- 2 cloves of garlic, chopped
- 6 tablespoons olive oil
- Sea salt and fresh ground pepper

Heat the oven to 350°F. In a stockpot filled with salted water, boil the potatoes for about 15 minutes until a fork can be inserted into one with slight resistance. In a bowl, combine the rosemary, garlic, olive oil, salt and pepper. Using a slotted spoon, transfer the potatoes to a cutting board and smash with the back of a large spoon, forming a disk. Place the disks on a cookie sheet lined with parchment paper and brush the flavored olive oil on top. Roast in the oven until golden and crispy, 15-20 minutes.

SERVES 6

Mashed Potatoes en Croûte

This is a really elegant way of serving mashed potatoes. I know it is a bit of a carbo-load but for a special occasion it is worth every rich bite. Don't even think about mashing the potatoes in the blender or food processor; giving in to such temptation will result in an inedible paste. You can mash the potatoes a little ahead of time, assemble the dish and then cook it just before serving.

6 to 8 large Idaho potatoes

½ cup milk

1 bay leaf

Pinch of nutmeg

4 tablespoons butter

¼ cup heavy cream

1 egg yolk

Sea salt and fresh ground pepper

2 sheets frozen puff pastry, (store bought) thawed at room temperature

4 tablespoons Parmesan, grated

Preheat the oven to 350°F. Peel and dice the potatoes and transfer to a large bowl of cold water to prevent them from discoloring. Bring a large pot of water to a boil. Add the potatoes, milk, bay leaf and salt. Cook until the potatoes are soft and very tender, about 25 minutes. Remove the bay leaf, drain the potatoes in a colander and return to the pot. Using a potato masher, mash the potatoes until soft and fluffy. Using a heavy-duty wire whisk, beat in the cream and butter. Season with nutmeg and salt to taste. Whisk in the egg yolk and set aside.

Line an 8-inch pie dish with one of the pastry sheets, allowing the edges to hang over the sides. Spoon the mashed potatoes into the dish and sprinkle with the Parmesan cheese. Top with the remaining sheet of puff pastry sheet and crimp the edges with a fork. Trim away excess pastry. Make a few decorative slits using a sharp knife and sprinkle the other two tablespoons Parmesan cheese on top of the pastry. Bake until the pastry has risen slightly and is golden, about 20 minutes. Serve hot, cutting into wedges.

SERVES 8

Potato Gratin with Salsa Española

An alternative to the classic potato gratin made with heavy cream, this version uses Salsa Española, page 111, a fragrant sauce made with onions and carrots. It is a staple in the Spanish kitchen, used on everything from meatballs to roasted chicken to turkey.

6 large potatoes, peeled and thinly sliced

2 cups Salsa Española, page 111

1 cup Parmesan cheese, grated

Butter for the dish

Heat the oven to 350°F. Bring a large pot of salted water to a boil. Add the potatoes and boil for 10 minutes, just until they start to change color. Drain them and dry them on a kitchen towel.

Butter a 4-quart oven-to-table dish and spread ⅓ of the potatoes on the bottom. Top with ⅓ of the Salsa Española. Continue alternating layers of potato and salsa, ending with a layer of potatoes. Top with the Parmesan and bake until the sauce is bubbly, the cheese golden and the potatoes cooked through, about 25 minutes. Serve warm.

SERVES 6 TO 8

Baby Bok Choy

*Swank Farms is a hydroponic grower of green produce in West Palm Beach. Every Saturday
I get my weekly allotment from them at the local farmer's market (the stand is right next to
Walter's Heirloom Tomatoes). Jody Swank always has intriguing vegetables that I have never
tasted before and loves to dish about how to cook them best. This baby bok choy is tender,
quick-cooking and incredibly flavorful. Sauté it with Roasted Garlic Dip & Marinade, page 115,
for a healthy side dish.*

4 tablespoons Roasted Garlic Dip & Marinade, page 115

4 bunches baby bok choy, sliced in half lengthwise

In a large sauté pan, heat the Roasted Garlic
Dip. Add the baby bok choy and sauté until
heated through, about 10 minutes. Transfer
to a platter and serve.

SERVES 8

Ginger Carrots

In Spanish cooking, ginger is mainly used in sweet rather than savory dishes. But I love its earthy, fiery flavor so much I try to use it as much as possible. Carrots seasoned with ginger are a revelation — a far cry from typically dull carrot offerings that mask the root vegetable's exquisite flavor. Presentation here is key, so cut the carrots in matchsticks, or even rounds for a pretty look.

4 tablespoons olive oil

1 3-inch piece of ginger, peeled and diced

1 clove of garlic, chopped

2 pounds carrots, cut into matchsticks or ¼-inch rounds

1 cup Vegetable Stock, page 103

1 tablespoon butter

½ cup parsley, chopped

In a large sauté pan, heat the olive oil over high heat. Add the ginger and garlic and sauté for a few seconds to release the aroma. Add the carrots and stir to coat. Add the broth and bring to a boil. Reduce the heat to medium-low and cover. Simmer until the carrots are tender, about 20 minutes. Remove the cover and reduce any liquid left in the pan. Stir in the butter and parsley and serve hot.

SERVES 6 TO 8

Golden Onions

The simplicity of this dish thrills me and for some reason it causes a similar reaction in male guests. I make this often when Vidalia onions are abundant at the market, but yellow onions and even large shallots work beautifully as well. Just make sure that all of the onions are the same size for even cooking.

8 medium yellow onions, peeled but left whole

1 pint Beef Stock, page 101

1 bay leaf

10 peppercorns

Preheat the oven to 350°F. In a large, deep lidded ovenproof dish, place the onions in a single layer. Pour in the stock to cover. Add the bay leaf and peppercorns. Cover and cook until the onions are very tender, about 1 hour. To serve, remove the bay leaf and peppercorns, transfer the onions to a decorative platter and pour the juices on top.

SERVES 8

Eggplant Bundles with Goat Cheese

Goat cheese is exceptional paired with eggplant, but goat cheese is not for everyone. If it is not your favorite, use mozzarella instead. If you want to make the bundles smaller, use zucchini strips instead of eggplant. And if you prefer coriander or mint, use it instead of basil.

- 2 to 3 medium-size eggplants, sliced lengthwise into long thin strips to make 16 pieces
- 1 pound firm goat cheese, cut into 8 slices
- 1 red tomato, cut into 8 slices
- 8 basil leaves, plus more for garnish
- 2 tablespoons olive oil
- 1 6-ounce can diced tomatoes

Heat the oven to 400°F. Line a cookie sheet with parchment paper. Arrange the eggplant slices on the parchment and bake until softened but still firm, about 10 minutes.

When cool enough to touch, place two eggplant slices in a cross pattern, overlapping each other. In the center, place a slice of goat cheese, topped by a slice of tomato and a basil leaf. Close the parcel, overlapping the eggplant slices. Secure with a toothpick and repeat with the remaining eggplant slices. Brush a little olive oil in an ovenproof dish. Place the bundles in the dish and pour the diced tomatoes over them. Bake until the cheese is softened and the eggplant is heated through. Garnish with basil leaves and serve warm.

SERVES 8

Sautéed Spinach with Raisins & Pinenuts

Spinach cooks down to nearly nothing so don't be concerned about the amount you need to make this dish. For a group of six hungry adults you will need at least 1 to 1½ pounds. Serve this earthy dish as an accompaniment to steaks or grilled shrimp. It is especially lovely served with Sea Bass with Salsa de Amontillado, page 151, since the sweet raisins in the spinach combine beautifully with the sweet wine in the fish dish.

4 tablespoons pine nuts

3 tablespoons olive oil

2 cloves of garlic, chopped

1½ pounds baby spinach leaves, stems removed

1 cup golden raisins

Sea salt and fresh ground pepper

Pinch of nutmeg

Heat a large sauté pan over medium-high heat. Add the pine nuts and sauté for a few minutes to release their aroma. Remove to a plate and set aside. In the same pan, add the olive oil and garlic and cook until the garlic begins to turn golden. Add the spinach by the handful, allowing it to wilt before adding the next handful. Add the raisins and pine nuts and season with salt, pepper and nutmeg. Transfer to a platter and serve.

SERVES 6

Garden Vegetables with Tarragon Butter

There is elegance in doing things simply, especially when it comes to vegetables. This dish is the perfect example. Its abundance makes serving platters appear full and generous and its versatility makes it a wonderful companion dish to myriad main courses, but it requires only five ingredients. Take them merely as suggestions: Use any combination of seasonal vegetables that you like.

3 pounds asparagus, ends trimmed

3 pounds green beans, ends trimmed

6 medium green or yellow zucchini, julienned

6 to 8 tablespoons salted butter

6 tablespoons fresh tarragon, chopped

Fill a shallow pan with 1 inch of salted water and bring to a boil. Add the asparagus and cook until just tender, about 15 minutes. Drain and place on a warm serving tray.

Fill the same shallow pan with 1 inch of salted water and bring to a boil. Add the beans and cook until tender, about 6 minutes. Drain and place on the warm serving tray. Repeat with the zucchini, cooking it for about 4 minutes.

In a small saucepan over medium-high heat, melt the butter. Add the tarragon leaves and warm for about 30 seconds, swirling the pan. Pour over the reserved vegetables and serve.

SERVES 10

Smashed Peas with Mint

My husband loves peas and I often make this as a side dish with roasted chicken, grilled lamb or steaks. Actually, it is good with almost anything! I cook the mint, peas and garlic all at the same time, then smash the peas to a thick consistency. It couldn't get any easier. If you're making it ahead of time, add a pat of butter and reheat over low heat.

1 pound fresh or frozen petit pois (small peas)

1 clove of garlic, roughly chopped

10 mint leaves, stems removed

Sea salt and fresh ground pepper

1 tablespoon butter

In a large saucepan filled with one inch of salted water, combine the peas, garlic and mint. Cook over medium-high heat until the peas are tender, about 5 minutes. Drain in a fine-mesh sieve. Transfer half the mixture to a blender or food processor and pulse for a few seconds. Return to the pan and mix with the remaining mixture. Add the butter and heat through over medium-high heat.

SERVES 6

Salt-Roasted Winter Vegetables

My favorite way of bringing incredible depth of flavor to vegetables is to roast them in the oven, which forces their natural sugars to caramelize. Add a bit of sea salt and pepper and serve them up! Use a combination of your favorite vegetables, roasting them on individual cookie sheets, then tossing them together for a gorgeous cornucopia of flavor to complement any main fish or meat. Each vegetable has a slightly different cooking time; so do keep an eye on the oven.

1 pound broccoli, florets trimmed and stems discarded

1 pound cauliflower, florets trimmed and stems discarded

1 pound baby carrots, halved lengthwise

4 tablespoons olive oil

Sea salt

Turn the oven to 400°F with three racks positioned equidistant from one another. Line three cookie sheets with parchment paper. Arrange the vegetables in one layer on each sheet. Drizzle 1 tablespoon olive oil on each sheet to coat the vegetables. Sprinkle with salt. Bake until soft and slightly charred around the edges, about 15 to 20 minutes. Transfer the vegetables to a large serving platter, toss with the remaining olive oil and serve.

SERVES 6 TO 8

Desserts

British-Style Custard, PAGE 190

Lemon Curd, PAGE 191

Ruby Red Grapefruit Foam, PAGE 192

Strawberry & Cointreau Sauce, PAGE 193

Orange Marmalade, PAGE 195

Isabel's Rice Pudding, PAGE 196

Bread & Butter Pudding with Pedro Ximénez, PAGE 197

Orange Bread & Butter Pudding, PAGE 198

Orange Pound Cake, PAGE 199

Torta de Santiago, PAGE 200

Chocolate Crêpe Cake, PAGE 202

Chocolate Mousse with Pedro Ximénez, PAGE 204

Warm Pineapple with Maple Syrup, PAGE 205

Apples Baked with Apricots, PAGE 207

Basil Ice Cream, PAGE 208

Banana Ice Cream, PAGE 209

I LIKE DESSERTS THAT REQUIRE MINIMAL FUSS. THERE IS NOTHING MORE PLEASING TO ME THAN A SIMPLE BOWL OF FRESH BERRIES

dressed up with a dollop of custard or whipped cream. Fruit is actually the main ingredient of most of my favorite desserts because it permits me to feel both virtuous and indulgent at the same time. When I am leaning more toward the indulgent, I like mixing fruit with liqueur and sugar to bring out its flavor. I also like the simplest of cooked desserts, like Rice Pudding and Torta de Santiago, a flourless almond cake beloved in Spain. Bread Pudding blends practicality (made a day ahead using leftover bread!) with outrageous richness (custard and sherry meet dark chocolate!) — who could resist such a treat?

To suit my no-fuss approach, the desserts in this chapter are designed for the busy home cook rather than the budding pastry chef. They call for easy-to-find ingredients and ask you to do very little work. Some are as simple as melting and stirring. The freezer or the oven will do the rest. Several are ideal for making ahead of time, such as Chocolate Crêpe Cake and the Rice and Bread Puddings. They all are delicious and make a splendid presentation at even the most formal dinner parties. No one will know how stress-free they were to create.

The key to making simple, flavorful desserts begins with the finest ingredients. I always use organic eggs and sugar, high-quality European chocolate, ripe seasonal fruit and heavy cream — the real stuff. I am not a fan of substituting ingredients with their low-fat cousins. I would much rather enjoy a small bite of something wholesome and real, than a whole portion of something that is made with chemically-based alternatives. After all, this is the European way, and it is how I grew up.

A great dessert is one that ends the meal on a sweet note. For everyday life, it can be as simple as the aforementioned bowl of fruit or as sublime as a scoop of store-bought vanilla ice cream with hot chocolate sauce. When I entertain, though, I do take a little more effort. Even so, I prefer desserts that can be made ahead. I seldom leave it for the last minute. It's not solely a matter of convenience; I have found that, although few things in life improve with age, desserts like bread pudding seem to do so, becoming richer and denser with a little extra time to mature.

On weekend mornings, with a house full of guests, I have even been known to begin my morning with such treats. The orange pound cake is delicious for breakfast, as are any of the fruit desserts, the first time around or as leftovers. I often double recipes and freeze cakes and tarts to warm up in the oven before serving. I keep marmalade and sweet sauces like Strawberry & Cointreau close at hand for impromptu meals. When you keep it simple, you really don't need a special occasion to enjoy a special dessert.

British-Style Custard

I adore this thick, sweetly aromatic sauce. It is sensational served on its own or as a filling for a pie or tart. It's even delicious spooned over vanilla ice cream—I'm not kidding. I often add mango, peach or strawberry purée for a different flavor. Add a bit of melted chocolate or caramel sauce to make it even more indulgent.

2 cups half-and-half

1 vanilla bean, split in half lengthwise

Rind of 1 lemon

4 large egg yolks

6 tablespoons sugar

In a saucepan over medium heat, combine the half-and-half, the scraped insides of the vanilla bean, and the lemon rind. Bring to a boil and immediately reduce the heat to low. Simmer for 10 minutes, remove from the heat and set aside to allow the flavors to develop. Let cool until no longer steaming.

In a separate bowl, combine the yolks and sugar until the sugar is dissolved. Incorporate the cream mixture in a slow stream, stirring well. Strain the sauce into a clean pot and cook over low heat, stirring constantly with a wooden spoon until the sauce is thick enough to coat the back of the spoon. Keep warm over a double boiler until ready to serve.

MAKES 2 1/2 CUPS

Lemon Curd

When I went to school outside London, we were allowed to bring jams, marmalades and spreads to have at teatime. Since then, I have been addicted to marmite, lemon curd and Bovril, a typically British spread. This basic recipe can be used as a filling for lemon pie and as a layer between slices of lemon pound cake. I use this to make Lemon Curd Ice Cream by mixing equal portions lemon curd and Greek yogurt and churning in an ice cream maker for 20 minutes. Freeze overnight but soften in the refrigerator for about one hour before serving.

2 whole eggs

2 egg yolks

½ cup sugar

½ cup unsalted chilled butter

Zest and juice of 2 lemons

In a metal bowl that fits over a double boiler, combine the eggs, yolks and sugar until smooth. Place over a pan of boiling water and add the butter, lemon juice and zest. Whisk until the mixture is thick enough to cover the back of a spoon. Strain into a jar and refrigerate until needed. It will keep for 2 weeks.

MAKES 1 CUP

Ruby Red Grapefruit Foam

This delicious sauce is Nouvelle Spanish cuisine: the trend of turning almost anything into a flavorful foam. I adore it served over a three-berry salad for an elegant dessert or alongside lemon or raspberry sorbet. I have experimented with other citrus without great results; the grapefruit has, by far, the perfect flavor and color.

1 cup Ruby Red grapefruit juice

2 tablespoons sugar

2 whole eggs

1 egg yolk

Combine the juice, sugar, eggs and yolk in the top of a double boiler and whisk with a hand-held electric mixer until light, fluffy and tripled in size, about 8 minutes. Chill in the refrigerator until ready to use.

MAKES 1 1/2 CUPS

Strawberry & Cointreau Sauce

This recipe came about by happenstance. I needed a quick sauce for a dessert that was a touch dry, had the ingredients in the pantry and a new sauce was born. This sweet and colorful sauce is ideal to serve over ice cream. I also use it to enhance fruit salad and serve it to garnish warm fruit pies. The bright red color makes desserts pop and the hint of Cointreau adds a wonderful ending for any meal. Use strawberries at their peak, or mix them with raspberries to make the sauce really red. I also make this sauce mid-winter with frozen fruit; just bring it to room temperature before blending.

2 pounds total raspberries and strawberries, washed and chopped, stems removed

2 tablespoons powdered sugar

Juice of ½ a lemon

4 tablespoons Cointreau (or more to taste)

In a blender, purée the raspberries and strawberries and the lemon juice with the powdered sugar and Cointreau. Strain through a medium-size sieve and refrigerate until ready to serve.

MAKES 2 CUPS

Orange Marmalade

My mother, who spends most of her time in Madrid and Sevilla, makes marmalade every year using bitter Seville oranges from a tree in the garden. It is by far the most fantastic marmalade I have ever tasted. The sweetness of the sugar combined with the very bitter oranges is divine. I have tried to replicate that bitterness by combining lemons and oranges to make this citrus marmalade. It keeps for several months in the refrigerator — a good thing, because I use it with abandon on morning toast, fillings for desserts and as a topping for pound cake.

6 thick-skinned oranges, such as Navel

2 thick-skinned lemons, such as Meyer

3 ½ pounds sugar

Fill a large stockpot with cold water and bring to a boil. Add the oranges and lemons and poach for about 30 minutes. Scoop out the fruit, dump the water and refill the pot with cold water. Bring to a boil, add the oranges and lemons and simmer for 60 minutes more, until the fruit is very soft. Using a slotted spoon, transfer the fruit to a cutting board to cool. Reserve the liquid.

When the fruit is cool enough to handle, use a vegetable peeler to remove just the peel of the oranges and lemons, taking care to leave the white pith behind and peeling over a bowl in order to collect the juices. Pass the pulp through a food mill and discard the pith, skins and any pits. Weigh the pulp; it should be about 2 pounds. Julienne the peel.

In a large stockpot, combine the sugar and 2 cups of the cooking liquid. Bring to a boil and simmer for 10 minutes until the syrup begins to turn light, light brown. Add the reserved pulp, bring to a boil and simmer again for another 10 to 15 minutes. Add the reserved julienned peel, bring to a boil and simmer again for another 15 to 20 minutes or until deep orange in color. As the syrup cooks it will bubble up; you can just blow gently on it to lower it and avoid spilling syrup in your stove. The marmalade is done when a drop of the syrup gels as it touches a plate.

Pour the mixture into sterilized Mason jars and keep, covered, in the refrigerator.

MAKES 8 CUPS

Isabel's Rice Pudding

Isabel was my great-grandmother's cook who then became my parents' cook when they got married. She was from Bilbao, the mecca of haute cuisine in Spain. Isabel brought with her an elegant and sophisticated cuisine, which graciously embellished the local Andalucian cooking. I barely remember her; in those days children were not allowed in the kitchen, but I do remember the back of her crisp white crisscross apron as she worked over the stove as well as many of the fabulous dishes she prepared for us.

6 ½ cups whole milk

4 tablespoons sugar

2 cinnamon sticks

Peel of 1 lemon, cut in wide strips

½ cup medium-grain white rice, such as Valencia

2 large eggs, separated

3 tablespoons sugar

½ teaspoon ground cinnamon for dusting

In a stockpot, combine 6 cups of the milk, sugar, cinnamon sticks and lemon peel. Bring to a boil. Add the rice, reduce the heat to low and simmer, stirring often, until the rice is tender and moist and most of the milk has been absorbed, about 1 hour. Discard the cinnamon sticks and lemon peel. Pour the rice pudding into a serving dish and refrigerate until well chilled.

In a small saucepan, heat the remaining ½ cup milk. In the top of a double boiler or in a metal bowl that can later fit into a larger pan, whisk the egg yolks with the sugar until the sugar is dissolved; stir in the hot milk. Place the bowl over a saucepan of simmering water and continue whisking until the sauce thickens to make a light crème anglaise, 6-7 minutes. Set aside.

In a small bowl, whisk the egg whites until peaks form. Fold the whites into the slightly cooled yolk mixture until frothy. Spread the sauce over the rice pudding and sprinkle with cinnamon.

SERVES 8 TO 10

Bread & Butter Pudding with Pedro Ximénez

I am addicted to bread-and-butter puddings of all kinds. I adore them for entertaining, especially when I'm expecting a crowd, since they are easy and quite economical to make. As with any dish, the better the ingredients, the better the outcome. Use the best bread available—artisanal is ideal. The key to making this pudding is to allow the bread to soak in the liquid long enough so that it seeps into it. The sweet, dark sherry imbues the bread with a distinctive flavor.

16 slices day-old raisin bread

½ cup (1 stick) butter, softened, plus more for the pan

1 cup Pedro Ximénez sherry

6 ounces dark chocolate, such as Lindt

1 cup milk

1 cup heavy cream

2 eggs

½ cup powdered sugar

1 teaspoon vanilla extract

1 teaspoon orange zest

Whipped cream for garnish

Preheat the oven to 350°F. Butter an 8-inch square baking dish. Toast the bread and spread butter on both sides. Arrange the bread in the baking dish so that it overlaps slightly. Drizzle with Pedro Ximénez and set aside.

In a saucepan over medium heat, combine the chocolate, milk and cream, stirring until melted. Set aside. In a large bowl, combine the eggs, sugar, vanilla and zest and whisk until frothy. Add the chocolate mixture and whisk to combine. Pour the mixture over the bread and let it sit for about 15 minutes until the bread has soaked up the liquid and has risen slightly.

Bake for 35 minutes until the top is crispy and the center still jiggles a little. Set aside to cool for about 10 minutes. Serve with a dollop of whipped cream.

SERVES 8

Orange Bread & Butter Pudding

Memories of boarding school flood back whenever I make this pudding. Not that we ever had this at school, but rather at friends' houses when I was invited for the weekend. It is the perfect dish to serve a crowd of hungry teenagers! Thick-cut Seville Orange Marmalade, page 195, is essential, as is giving the bread adequate time to absorb the liquid.

1 ½ baguettes

Butter for preparing the baking dish

½ cup golden raisins

1 pint whole milk

12 eggs

1 cup sugar

Zest of 1 lemon

1 teaspoon vanilla extract

Peel of 1 orange, julienned

2 cups Orange Marmalade, page 195

Preheat the oven to 350°F. Trim away the top crust of the baguette and slice into ¼-inch slices. Butter the slices on both sides and spread the marmalade on one side only. Arrange the slices, marmalade side up, at a slight angle in a rectangular oven dish. Sprinkle raisins on top.

Combine the milk, eggs, sugar, lemon zest, vanilla and orange essence in a large saucepan. Stir well. Place the mixture over high heat and bring to a boil, stirring constantly. Reduce the heat and simmer for about 4 minutes, to allow the flavors to develop. Remove the lemon zest. Pour the mixture over the bread slices and let soak for about 20 minutes, pressing down the bread with your fingers so it is covered with the egg mixture. Sprinkle orange peel on top. Cover with foil and bake 30 minutes, then uncover and bake an additional 30 minutes, until the top turns golden.

In a small saucepan, warm the remaining marmalade until thin and pour over the pudding while still hot. Serve with orange-scented whipped cream.

SERVES 8 TO 10

Orange Pound Cake

The simplicity of this pound cake allows for all sorts of additions and substitutions. I adore changing things around and this recipe lets me do just that. I have made it with lemons instead of oranges, soaked it in rum or Cointreau, added almond or vanilla extract and played with the toppings. Besides orange marmalade, I have served it with lemon curd, melted honey and even — in a total fit of "I have nothing in the fridge" — Nutella, a hazelnut-chocolate spread, much to the delight of children and adults alike.

1 thin-skinned orange, such as Valencia

½ cup (1 stick) butter

2 cups self-rising flour

2 cups sugar

4 eggs

Pinch of salt

1 cup Orange Marmalade, page 195

Preheat the oven to 350°F. Butter an 8-inch loaf pan.

Chop the orange and remove the seeds, leaving the skin on (trust me). Place in a food processor. Add the butter, flour, sugar, salt and eggs and purée until the batter is light and smooth, about 3 minutes.

Pour the batter into the prepared loaf pan and bake for about 40 minutes until golden or a skewer, inserted in the center, comes out clean. Set aside in the pan until cool enough to handle. Turn out onto a wire rack to cool completely.

In a small bowl, melt the orange marmalade and pour over the loaf allowing the syrup to dribble down the sides. Cut into ½-inch-thick slices and serve.

SERVES 8

Torta de Santiago

Legend has it that medieval pilgrims made this flourless almond tart on their way to Santiago in honor of the patron saint of Spain. How the pilgrims made it without modern electrical appliances, I don't know, but it is easy to make today using a coffee grinder to grind the almonds until they resemble coarse sand. This tart is remarkably moist and sensationally lemony. Serve it right out of the oven, with a scoop of vanilla ice cream or Strawberry Cointreau Sauce, page 193.

½ pound almonds, preferably peeled

1 cup sugar

6 extra large eggs, separated

Pinch of salt

2 tablespoons grated lemon zest

1 teaspoon ground cinnamon

Powdered sugar for garnish

Preheat the oven to 350°F. Butter and flour a 9-inch springform pan. Using a clean coffee grinder, grind the almonds to a fine consistency, making sure there are no lumps (you might want to strain the almonds through a medium-size sieve).

In a large bowl, combine the egg whites with a pinch of salt and two tablespoons of the sugar and whisk until soft peaks form. In another bowl, combine the egg yolks, the remaining sugar and the cinnamon and whip using an electric hand-held mixer until it has doubled in size and is pale in color. Stir in the almonds and grated lemon zest. Fold in the egg white mixture, one spoonful at a time. Pour into the pan and bake for 45 minutes. Set aside to cool. Place the powdered sugar in a fine-mesh sieve and tap over the cake to decorate.

SERVES 8 TO 10

HOW TO FRY COOKIES

Heat ½ inch of olive oil in a pan until just smoking. Make sandwiches using butter cookies and
jam. Place in the hot oil for 30 seconds and cook
on the other side. Drain on paper towels and
sprinkle powdered sugar on top. Serve hot.

Chocolate Crêpe Cake

This sensational cake looks difficult to make but it is actually very easy. If you can make a pancake, you can make a crêpe. Do invest in a crêpe pan; it does make life a bit easier. The cake needs to sit in the fridge overnight to become firm, so it's a good make-ahead party cake. The batter for this recipe fits exactly into a standard blender — you will need to double it to make enough crêpes to fill a 9-inch round springform pan. Serve it with a dollop of orange-scented whipped cream on the side. To make it, simply add orange zest or extract to whipped cream.

For the chocolate sauce (double this recipe for a 9-inch cake):

10 ounces dark, semisweet or bittersweet chocolate, such as Lindt

3 tablespoons unsalted butter

½ cup milk

½ cup heavy cream

½ cup powdered sugar

½ cup brandy or rum (optional)

For the crêpes (double this recipe for a 9-inch cake):

1 ⅔ cups flour

1 tablespoon powdered sugar

3 whole eggs

3 egg yolks

2 cups milk

Pinch of salt

2 tablespoon grated orange zest

2 tablespoons unsalted butter, melted, plus more for the pan

Whipped cream flavored with orange extract for garnish

Make the chocolate sauce: In the top of a double boiler, combine the chocolate, butter, milk, cream, sugar and brandy (if using). Stir over medium heat until smooth. Remove from the heat and set aside to cool slightly.

Make the crêpes: Combine the flour, sugar, eggs, yolks, milk and salt in a blender until smooth. Set aside for about 30 minutes. Stir in 2 tablespoons melted butter and blend again.

Melt 1 tablespoon butter in a 9-inch nonstick crêpe pan (the same size as the springform pan you will be using). Swirl in enough crêpe batter to just cover the pan in a thin layer, about ½ cup. Cook until the crêpe separates easily from the pan, about 1 minute, and flip to cook on the other side for about 30 seconds. Add more butter to the pan as needed and continue cooking crêpes until you have about 20. As you cook them, keep them separated with parchment paper.

Butter the bottom and sides of a 9-inch spring-form pan. Place one crêpe on the bottom, spoon 1 tablespoon chocolate sauce on it and spread with the back of the spoon. Repeat with the remaining crêpes, ending with chocolate sauce. Cover and chill in the refrigerator for at least 2 hours or overnight. Cover remaining chocolate sauce and refrigerate.

When ready to serve, heat the chocolate sauce in a small saucepan over medium-low heat. Unmold the cake onto a decorative platter. Pour the sauce over the cake and spread in an even layer, allowing some of the sauce to trickle down the sides.

SERVES 8 TO 10

Chocolate Mousse with Pedro Ximénez

Pedro Ximénez is a sweet dessert sherry that I use in nearly everything! Chocolate brings out its deep smoky flavor and the wonderful sweetness of grapes dried in the sun. This mousse is not for children, but grownups will devour it in no time.

10.5 ounces chocolate, about 3 bars Lindt semisweet chocolate

4 tablespoons butter

1 cup heavy whipping cream

4 eggs

1 cup powdered sugar

1 cup Pedro Ximénez sherry

In a small saucepan over a double boiler, melt the chocolate and butter, stirring, until smooth. Remove from the heat.

Using an electric mixer, whisk the heavy cream in a large bowl until stiff. In a clean large bowl, separate the eggs from the whites. Beat the egg whites until stiff. In another bowl combine the egg yolks, Pedro Ximénez and the sugar until light and frothy. Slowly incorporate the chocolate mixture, beating well after each addition. Using a rubber spatula, fold in the whipped cream, followed by the egg whites. Pour into a decorative dessert bowl and refrigerate until ready to serve.

SERVES 8

Warm Pineapple with Maple Syrup

Pineapple, the symbol of hospitality, is grilled in this dessert with maple syrup, pecans and rum. The combination is fantastic and the presentation can be sublime. I like serving food in large communal platters to give a feeling of abundance and generosity, the perfect way to present this dessert. I have also served it using the shell of the pineapple as a decorative vessel. I often serve purchased gourmet cookies with this as well. Add other fruits as desired, but if serving this in the summer, make sure they can stand up to the heat.

1 pineapple, peeled, cored and sliced into ½-inch rounds

4 tablespoons brown sugar

4 tablespoons rum

6 tablespoons butter

1 cup real maple syrup

½ cup pecans, roughly chopped

2 tablespoons rum, optional

1 pint vanilla ice cream

In a bowl, sprinkle the sugar and rum over the pineapple slices and marinate for at least 30 minutes (or while you set the table).

In a sauté pan, melt 2 tablespoons of the butter and, working in batches, sauté the pineapple slices until slightly golden brown, adding more butter as needed. Transfer to a serving platter.

After the last pineapple slice is done, pour the maple syrup into the pan. Use a wooden spoon to incorporate it with the juices and bits of butter. Remove the pan from the heat and add the rum (if using). Pour the warm syrup over the pineapple slices, scatter the pecans over and serve with a dollop of vanilla ice cream.

SERVES 6

Apples Baked with Apricots

During the Christmas holidays, I fill apples with mincemeat and serve them baked with brandy butter. But for the spring or summer, I make a lighter version of the filling with dried fruits. Use baking apples that are unblemished and give them a good rinse to remove the waxy layer if they are not organic.

8 Golden Delicious apples, cored, with bottoms intact

16 dried apricots

½ cup golden raisins

6 tablespoons Calvados (apple brandy)

2 tablespoons butter

6 tablespoons sugar

Vanilla ice cream or heavy cream

Preheat the oven to 350°F. Place the apples in a baking dish and fill each apple with apricots and raisins. Divide the Calvados evenly among them and dot each with butter. Sprinkle with sugar. Fill the pan with about ½ inch of water and bake until the apples are soft and cooked through, 30-40 minutes.

Serve with vanilla ice cream or heavy cream.

SERVES 8

Basil Ice Cream

This is my favorite dessert in the summertime when my basil plant has grown into a small tree. It is also a great recipe to have in your repertoire for a quick, no-cook dessert that will impress your friends to no end. Experiment with different types of basil, like lemon or cinnamon.

I serve this ice cream with a simple fresh berry salad or hot chocolate sauce. The color combination is spectacular!

1.75 quarts vanilla ice cream (preferably Edy's)

8 cups basil leaves, without stems

Thaw the vanilla ice cream by leaving it at room temperature until it is easy to stir but not totally melted.

Fill a small saucepan with water and bring to a boil. Submerge the basil leaves in the water to blanch, about 5 seconds. Remove with a slotted spoon and pat dry with a paper towel. Combine 1 cup ice cream with the basil leaves in a blender and purée until it is smooth and the color is even. Transfer to a bowl and mix with the remaining ice cream. Pour final mixture into a decorative mold and freeze for at least 2 hours before serving.

SERVES 8 TO 10

Banana Ice Cream

Greek yogurt has totally revolutionized my dessert repertoire. It is healthy, light and incredibly easy to use. It can be heated, maintains its shape and gives great flavor to mousses, cakes and ice creams, as in this basic recipe where the yogurt becomes the no-cooking base for an elegant and delicious ice cream. I love to scoop it into balls, put them in a dessert bowl and refreeze them. Sometimes I freeze it in a loaf pan, unmold it and garnish with pecans and walnuts.

An alternative to this version is to mix the yogurt with 1 cup puréed strawberries, blueberries and raspberries. Strain the purée through a medium-size sieve to remove seeds and blend with the yogurt, sugar, cream and lemon juice. I call this version Three Berry Yogurt Ice Cream.

3 soft but not overly ripe bananas

2 cups plain Greek-style yogurt

1 cup heavy cream

1 cup sugar

Juice of ½ a lemon

Working in batches, combine the bananas, yogurt, heavy cream, sugar and lemon juice in a blender and purée until smooth. Pour into an ice cream machine and follow the manufacturer's directions. Freeze until ready to serve.

SERVES 8

GUIDE TO FRIENDS

Sharing recipes is like sharing friends: The good ones are always there when you need them. I am fortunate to have lots of both. Here is my list of companies, suppliers and friends that make my life easier. I hope you make them yours too.

EXTENDA The Andalucian export office from Spain; anything from the best olive oils to the most beautiful ceramics. www.extenda.es

VALDERRAMA Monovarietal olive oils from Spain, each with a distinct flavor. They also have the most delicious truffle oils. www.valderrama.es

LUSTAU One of the oldest sherry companies in Spain. I adore their Pedro Ximénez, Fine Fino sherry and wine vinegars. www.lustau.com

ALL CLAD Fantastic pots and pans which I use everyday. The crêpe pan is like my third arm. www.allclad.com

JENNIFER GARRIGUES In Palm Beach, Jenny's shop is a treasure trove of antiques, furniture and decorative accessories. A must see. www.jennifergarrigues.com

MIMI McMAKIN A wonderful shop full of Palm Beach style and charm. Mimi carries everything chic for the house. www.kembleinteriors.com

VIVI'S PALM BEACH Oldest stationery in Palm Beach, they carry the most wonderful papers. Tim Carew knows as much about etiquette and protocol as Mrs. Post. www.vivispalmbeach.com

BLONDE DESIGNS Kristin and Angie design beautiful custom stationery for every aspect of life, from weddings to personal papers. www.blonde-designs.com

STUBBS & WOOTTON Needlepoint slippers and velvet shoes, they make standing on my feet all day a pleasure; further more, they look great. www.stubbsandwootton.com

MYFOODMYHEALTH.COM A new website with amazing information on food and cooking for specific health problems. www.myfoodmyhealth.com

INDEX

NOTE: Page numbers in *italics* refer to photographs.

A

Aïoli (Alioli), 107

Ana Arias' Little Bits Salad, 135

Apples Baked with Apricots, *207*

B

Baby Bok Choy, *177*

Banana Ice Cream, *209*

Basil Ice Cream, 208

Beef Stock, 101

Boneless Leg of Lamb a la Moruna, 162

Bread

    Bread & Butter Pudding with Pedro Ximénez, 197

    Creamy Garlic Soup, 88

    Good Old-Fashioned Meatloaf, *160*

    Orange Bread & Butter Pudding, 198

    Tomato & Jamón Serrano Toasts with Truffle Oil, 69

Bread & Butter Pudding with Pedro Ximénez, 197

Breasts of Chicken with Sage & Serrano, *157*

Bullshot, *47*

C

Caipirinha & Caipiroska, *49*

Carajillo, 46

Champagne & Pomegranate, 52

Chicken in Champagne Sauce, 156

Chicken Stock, 100

Chocolate Crêpe Cake, *202*

Chocolate Mousse with Pedro Ximénez, 204

Chorizo Empanadas, 64

Clams with Chorizo, *61*

Cornish Game Hens with Lemon & Rosemary, 158

Creamy Garlic Soup, 88

Curry Mayonnaise "Al Fresco", 109

Custard, British-Style, 190

D

Duck Magret & Warm Onion Salad, 134

E

Egg

    Huevos a la Flamenca, 146

    Huevos al Plato, 144

    Huevos de la Casa, 145

    Poached Egg Salad with Red Wine Sauce, 124

    Potato Tortilla with Onion & Chorizo, *66*

    Three Vegetable Tortilla, 143

Eggless Mayonnaise, 108

Eggplant

    Eggplant Bundles with Goat Cheese, *181*

    Eggplant, Béchamel & Tomato Gratin, 142

    Fried Eggplant with Honey, 63

    Huevos al Plato, 144

    Moussaka, 163

    Shrimp & Eggplant Bundles, 62

    Sopa de Picadillo, 94

    Vegetable Tortillas, 143

Eggplant Bundles with Goat Cheese, *181*

Eggplant, Béchamel and Tomato Gratin , 142

Ensaladilla Rusa (Russian Salad), 137

Everyday Vegetable Purée, 90

F

Fish & Shellfish

    Clams with Chorizo, *61*

Fussilli with Shrimp, Garlic & Lemon, 169

Garlic Shrimp, 60

Gypsy Rice, 147

Mussels in Curry Sauce, 150

Porch House Striped Sea Bass, 152

Prawn & Potato Salad with Warm Mustard Sauce, 136

Prawns en Papillote, *148*

Sea Bass with Salsa de Amontillado, 151

Shrimp & Crab Curry Chowder, 95

Shrimp & Eggplant Bundles, 62

Shrimp Fideoada, 168

Smoked Salmon Soup, *87*

Fresh Herb Sauce & Marinade, *113*

Fried Eggplant with Honey, 63

Fruits

Ana Aria's Little Bits Salad, 135

Apples Baked with Apricots, *207*

Banana Ice Cream, *209*

Lemon Curd, 191

Orange & Red Onion Salad, *123*

Orange Marmalade, *195*

Orange Pound Cake, 199

Preserved Lemons, *105*

Ruby Red Grapefruit Foam, 192

Sangría de Verdad, *54*

Serrano-Wrapped Figs with Blue Cheese, 68

Strawberry & Cointreau Sauce, *193*

Strawberry & Tomato Gazpacho, 80

Tomato & Plum Gazpacho, 79

Vodka & Watermelon, *52*

Warm Pineapple with Maple Syrup, 205

Fusilli with Shrimp, Garlic & Lemon, 169

G

Garden Vegetables with Tarragon Butter, 183

Garlic Shrimp, 60

Gazpachos

Lettuce, 81

Strawberry & Tomato, 80

Tomato & Plum, 79

Tomato & Roasted Beet, 82

Yellow, 78

Ginger Carrots, 178

Gnocchi a la Romana, *171*

Golden Onions, 179

Good Old-Fashioned Meatloaf, *160*

Gypsy Rice, 147

H

How to Fry Cookies, 201

How to Peel Tomatoes, 133

How to Roast Peppers, 126

How to Make Simple Syrup, 50

Homemade Mayonnaise, 106

Huevos a la Flamenca, 146

Huevos al Plato (Baked Eggs), 144

Huevos de la Casa, 145

I

Isabel's Rice Pudding, 196

L

Lamb Chops with Fresh Herb Sauce, 159

Layered Curried Chicken Salad, 130

Lemon Curd, 191

Lettuce Gazpacho, 81

INDEX

M

Mashed Potatoes en Croûte, *174*

Mayonnaise

    Alïoli, 107

    Curry "Al Fresco", 109

    Eggless, 108

    Homemade, 106

    Mint, 108

    Mustard & Lemon, 107

    Salsa Andaluza (Pink), 109

    Truffle Oil, 107

Mayonnaise with Mint, 108

Mayonnaise with Truffle Oil, 107

Meats

    Boneless Leg of Lamb a la Moruna, 162

    Good Old-Fashioned Meatloaf, *160*

    Lamb Chops with Fresh Herb Sauce, 159

    Meatballs with Mint, 70

    Moussaka, 163

    Pork Tenderloin with Pedro Ximénez & Cabrales Cheese, 65

Meatballs with Mint, 70

Moussaka, 163

Mushroom Cream Sauce, British Style, 112

Mushroom Soup with Tarragon & Truffle Oil, *92*

Mussels with Curry Sauce, 150

Mustard & Lemon Mayonnaise, 107

O

Orange & Red Onion Salad, *123*

Orange Bread & Butter Pudding, 198

Orange Marmalade, *195*

Orange Pound Cake, 199

P

Pastas & Rice

    Fussili with Shrimp, Garlic & Lemon, 169

    Gnocchi a la Romana, *171*

    Gypsy Rice, 147

    Isabel's Rice Pudding, 196

    Spaghetti with Fresh Tomato & Basil, 172

Patatas Bravas (Fiery Potatoes), 72

Pink Béchamel Sauce, 110

Poached Egg Salad with Red Wine Sauce, 124

Porch House Striped Sea Bass, 152

Pork Tenderloin with Pedro Ximénez & Cabrales Cheese, 65

Potato

    Ensaladilla Rusa, 137

    Everyday Vegetable Purée, 90

    Layered Curried Chicken Salad, 130

    Mashed Potatoes en Croûte, *174*

    Patatas Bravas, 72

    Potato Crisps, 71

    Potato Gratin with Salsa Española, 176

    Potato Tortilla with Onion & Chorizo, *66*

    Prawn & Potato Salad with Warm Mustard Sauce, 136

    Smoked Salmon Soup, *87*

    Smashed Potatoes with Rosemary, 173

Potato Crisps, 71

Potato Gratin with Salsa Española, 176

Potato Tortilla with Onion & Chorizo, *66*

Prawn & Potato Salad with Mustard Sauce, 136

Prawns en Papillote, 148

Preserved Lemons, 104

Poultry

    Breasts of Chicken with Sage & Serrano, *157*

    Chicken in Champagne Sauce, 156

Chicken Tagine, Olives & Lemons, *155*

Cornish Game Hens with Lemon & Rosemary, 158

Duck Magret & Warm Onion Salad, 134

Layered Curried Chicken Salad, 130

Saucy Contessa Chicken, 153

R

Red Pepper & Red Onion Salad, *126*

Red Wine Sauce, 125

Roasted Garlic Dip & Marinade, *115*

Romaine Hearts with Crispy Garlic, *129*

Ruby Red Grapefruit Foam, 192

S

Salsa Andaluza (Pink Mayonnaise), 109

Salsa Española, 111

Salt-Roasted Winter Vegetables, 185

Sangría de Verdad, *54*

Saucy Contessa Chicken, 153

Sautéed Spinach with Raisins & Pine Nuts, 182

Sea Bass with Salsa de Amontillado, 151

Senegalese Soup, British Style, 86

Serrano-Wrapped Figs with Blue Cheese, 68

Shellfish Stock, 102

Shrimp & Crab Curry Chowder, 95

Shrimp & Eggplant Bundles, 62

Shrimp Fideoada, 168

Smashed Peas with Mint, 184

Smashed Potatoes with Rosemary, 173

Smoked Salmon Soup, *87*

Sopa de Picadillo, 94

Southampton Iced Tea, 51

Southside, 50

Spaghetti with Fresh Tomato & Basil, 172

Spanish Onion Soup, 89

Spiced Walnuts, 73

Strawberry & Cointreau Sauce, *193*

Strawberry & Tomato Gazpacho, 80

T

Tagine of Chicken, Olives & Lemon, *155*

Tinto de Verano, 55

Tomato & Jamón Serrano Toasts with Truffle Oil, 69

Tomato & Plum Gazpacho, 79

Tomato & Roasted Beet Gazpacho, 82

Tomato Jam, Moroccan Style, 117

Tomato Salad, *132*

Tomato Sauce (Salsa de Tomate), *116*

Torta de Santiago, 200

V

Vegetable Stock, 103

Vegetables with Tarragon Butter, 183

Vodka & Watermelon, *52*

W

Wake-Up-Call, The, 55

Warm Pineapple with Maple Syrup, 205

Watercress Soup, 84

White & Green Asparagus Soup, 83

Y

Yellow Gazpacho, 78

Z

Zucchini & Blue Cheese Salad, 122

Zucchini Soup, 85